Charles Joseph Leslie

Historical Records of the Family of Leslie from 1067 to 1868-69

Collected from public records and authentic private sources. Vol. 1

Charles Joseph Leslie

Historical Records of the Family of Leslie from 1067 to 1868-69
Collected from public records and authentic private sources. Vol. 1

ISBN/EAN: 9783337218867

Printed in Europe, USA, Canada, Australia, Japan

Cover: Foto ©ninafisch / pixelio.de

More available books at **www.hansebooks.com**

HISTORICAL RECORDS

OF THE

FAMILY OF LESLIE

Printed by R. Clark,
FOR
EDMONSTON & DOUGLAS, EDINBURGH.

LONDON . . .	HAMILTON, ADAMS, AND CO.
CAMBRIDGE . .	MACMILLAN AND CO
DUBLIN . . .	M'GLASHAN AND GILL.
GLASGOW . . .	JAMES MACLEHOSE.

HISTORICAL RECORDS

OF THE

FAMILY OF LESLIE

FROM

1067 TO 1868-9

Collected from Public Records and Authentic Private Sources

BY

COLONEL LESLIE, K.H.

OF BALQUHAIN

VOL. I.

EDINBURGH
EDMONSTON AND DOUGLAS
1869

[*All rights reserved.*]

PREFACE.

HITHERTO the history of the Family of Leslie has been known chiefly through the medium of the *Laurus Leslæana*, published at Gratz, in 1692, by the Rev. William Leslie, younger son of Patrick, Count Leslie, fifteenth Baron of Balquhain. This work, though compiled with great industry, is yet not exempt from much deficiency and many inaccuracies. It is found to be pretty correct as far as relates to the Leslies of Balquhain and the Counts Leslie in Germany; but with regard to some of the generations of the original family of Leslie, and the origin of the noble house of Rothes, the *Laurus* is entirely wrong, as is proved by authentic charters and other documents now existing.

Crawford's, Douglas', and other *Peerages*, are very deficient and erroneous in many particulars, occasioned, no doubt, from the authors not having had the advantage of access to the many valuable public and private documents now brought to light by the extensive research and the inquiring spirit of modern antiquarians.

For the Historical Records of the Family of Leslie now attempted, use has been carefully made not only of those works of our various antiquarian clubs, but, in addition, recourse has been had to the valuable stores laid up, as well in the repositories of the public records as in private charter-rooms. By the materials thence collected many errors contained in the *Laurus Leslæana*, and in the various *Peerages*, have been corrected, and many deficiencies have been supplied. Wherever there has been occasion to differ from the *Laurus Leslæana* and the *Peerages*, the authority for the difference has been given.

Among the public works consulted, besides the publications of the various antiquarian clubs, may be particularised the *Registrum Magni Sigilli*, the *Acta Dominorum Concilii*, and Robertson's *Index of Missing Charters*. The public repositories which have been searched are the Advocates' Library and the General Register House, Edinburgh. From unpublished charters many valuable and interesting facts have been obtained. Access has been had to private charter-rooms, including those of Balquhain, the Earls of Rothes, Pitcaple, and Leith-hall, which latter family is now in possession of the ancient barony of Leslie. From these various sources the present Historical

Records of the Family of Leslie have been compiled, showing the descent of the family from 1067 to 1868. It is hoped that these records will be found correct, as far as authentic information can at present be obtained. Many errors and omissions have been rectified and supplied. Still there remain historical points to be ascertained, which further research may elucidate.

The author does not profess to be a historian. He presents this work to the public only as a collection of the most authentic documents relating to the history of the family of Leslie. He trusts that some one more competent than himself may be induced to write a history of the family.

The annals of great families, when divested of fable, besides being interesting to the genealogist and to those parties more immediately concerned, frequently form not unimportant contributions to general history. Some such benefit as this may naturally be expected from the annals of the Leslies, who have done the state some service in their day, both in the senate and in the field; members of the family having been engaged in almost all the important transactions of their time, both at home and abroad, distinguishing themselves as military heroes, eminent ecclesiastics, and renowned statesmen. Indeed, this family had the distinguished honour of producing a succession of great men, who, by their prudence, valour, and learning, raised themselves to the highest offices of honour in this and in foreign countries. Five generals of the name of Leslie commanded the armies of four different nations—Scotland, Germany, Sweden, and Russia—nearly all at the same time. Count Walter and Count James Leslie of the Balquhain family were Field-Marshals in the Imperial service, and commanded the Imperial armies on several occasions. Alexander Leslie, Earl of Leven, descended from the Kininvie branch of the Balquhain family, was a Field-Marshal in the Swedish army under Gustavus Adolphus, and afterwards commanded the forces of the Covenanters in Scotland. David Leslie, Lord Newark, of the Rothes family, also served in the Swedish army under Gustavus Adolphus, and was appointed Lieutenant-General of the Scottish army sent by the Parliament to assist the English Parliament against King Charles I. He afterwards held the same rank under King Charles II., who created him Lord Newark. Sir Alexander Leslie of Auchintoul, of the family of Leslie of Crichie, a branch of the Balquhain family, went to Russia, where, after long and great services rendered to the Duke of Muscovy, he became a general, and was made Governor of Smolensko. Besides these field-marshals and generals, there were many colonels and officers of inferior rank of the name of. Leslie serving at home and abroad.

The family has not been less distinguished in more peaceable pursuits—witness John Leslie, Bishop of Ross, the great statesman and historian, and the devoted adherent of the unfortunate Mary Queen of Scots; John, Duke of Rothes, statesman and ambassador in the reign of King Charles II.; William Leslie, son of William Leslie, fifth Laird of Warthill, who went to Germany and became Prince Bishop of Laybach, and a Privy Councillor of the Empire; the Right Rev. Dr. Henry Leslie, of the Rothes family, who was Protestant Bishop of Down in 1635, and of Meath in 1650; the Right Rev. Dr. Robert Leslie, also of the Rothes family, who was successively Protestant Bishop of Dromore, Raphoe, and Clogher; the Right Rev. Dr. John Leslie, of the Wardis family, who was Protestant Bishop of Orkney, of Dromore, of Clogher, and of Raphoe; the Right Rev. Dr. John Leslie, nephew of the preceding, who was Bishop of Dromore and of Clogher; another Right Rev. Dr. John Leslie, also of the Wardis family, who was Bishop of Dromore in 1812, and Bishop of Elphin in 1830; Sir John Leslie, Professor of Natural Philosophy in the University of Edinburgh, who died 3d November 1832, and who was known in this country and all over Europe as one of the most eminent characters of the age, having few rivals as a mathematician and philosopher, as a profound and accomplished scholar, and as a proficient in general literature and in history, and many other branches of knowledge.

AUTHORITIES consulted by COLONEL CHARLES LESLIE, K.H., twenty-sixth Baron of Balquhain, when collecting Records for the History of the Family of Leslie, 1833-1868.

Laurus Leslæana, by the Rev. William Leslie. *Gratz*, 1692.

De Origine Moribus et Rebus Gestis Scotorum, Authore Joanne Leslaeo, Episcopo Rossensi. *Romæ*, M.D.LXXVIII.

A Restitution of Decayed Intelligence in Antiquities concerning the most noble and renowned English Nation, by the studie and trauaile of Richard Verstegan. *Antwerp*, 1605.

Martin of Clermont's Genealogical Tables and Collections. *Advocates' Library, Edinburgh*, 1712.

Macfarlane's Collections.

Crawford's Peerage. *Edinburgh*, 1716.

Douglas' Peerage.

Douglas' Baronage.

Playfair's Family Antiquities.

Burke's Peerage.

Burke's Extinct Peerage.

Burke's Landed Gentry.

Riddell on Scotch Peerage and Consistorial Law. 1842.

Riddell's Remarks on Scotch Peerage Law. 1833.

Dugdale's Monasticon.

Nisbet's Heraldry. *Edinburgh*, 1722.

Collin's Peerage.

AUTHORITIES.

Debret's Peerage.
Lodge's Peerage.
Chambers' Biographical Dictionary. *Glasgow*, 1835.
Bayley's Biographical Dictionary.
Northcote's Historical Dictionary.
Betham's Genealogical Tables. *London*, 1795.
Anderson's Genealogical Tables.
Hubner's Genealogical Tables. *Leyden*, 1729.
Tree of the Royal Family of Scotland. *Edinburgh*, 1793.
Buchanan's History of Scotland.
Tytler's History of Scotland.
Spottiswood's Collections.
Hume's History of the Douglas Family.
Andrew Stewart's History of the Stewarts.
Abercromby's Martial Achievements.
Genealogy of the Family of Forbes, from the account of Mr. Mathew Lumsden of Tulliekerne, written in 1580. Published at Inverness 1819.
Kennedy's Annals of Aberdeen.
Records of the County of Aberdeen, by John Grant Leslie, Esq., Sheriff-clerk of Aberdeen.
Orem's History of Aberdeen.
Book of Bon-accord.
Theatre of Mortality, Aberdeen.
Rev. James Gordon's History.
Spalding's History of the Troubles in Scotland.
Old Statistical Account of Aberdeenshire.
New Statistical Account of Aberdeenshire.
Shaw's History of Moray. 1775 and 1827.
Sir Robert Sibbald's History of Fife.
Lives of Illustrious Scotchmen.

AUTHORITIES.

Crawford's Lives of State Officers.
The Complaint of Scotland.
Sir James Balfour of Denmylne's Historical Collections. 1824.
Sir James Dalrymple's Collections.
Haddington Collections.
Sir George Mackenzie's Collections.
Lord Hailes' Annals.
Lord Lindsay's Lives of the Lindsays.
Keith's Historical Catalogue.
Rinnuccini's Life of Father Archangel, the Scotch Capuchin.
Sir Robert Gordon's History of the Sutherland Family.
Registrum Magni Sigilli. 1306–1424.
Chamberlain's Rolls.
Robertson's Index of Missing Charters. *Edinburgh*, 1798.
Inquest of Retours Abbreviate.
Inquisitiones Generales.
Inquisitiones Speciales.
Acta Dominorum Concilii.
Notes of Charters in Library of Writers to the Signet, Edinburgh.
The Ragman Rolls, 1291–1296. Bannatyne Club.
Charters of Leslie of Leslie.
Charters of the Earls of Rothes.
Charters of Leslie, Barons of Balquhain.
Charters of Leslie, Barons of Pitcaple.
Charters of the Earls of Errol.
Charters of the Earls of Strathmore.
Charters of the Lords Panmure.
Charters of Rose of Kilravock.

List of Pollable Persons in Aberdeenshire, 1696;
published 1844.
Proceedings for and against the Counts Leslie in the Court of Session and House of Lords. 1739–1762.
Extracts from the Archives du Royaume. Paris.
Oliver's Biography of Scotch Jesuits. *London*, 1845.
Registrum Moraviense. Bannatyne Club.
Chartulary of Aberdeen.
Chartulary of Ross.
Chartulary of Cupar.
Chartulary of St. Andrews.
Chartulary of Lindores.
Chartulary of Arbroath.
Colonel Mitchell's Life of Wallenstein.
Itinerarivm R. D. Thomae Carve Tripperariensis, Sacellanimaioris in fortissimâ juxta et Nobilissima Legione Strenuissimi Domini Colonelli D. Walteri Deveroux sub Sac. Caesar. Maiestate stipendia merentis, cum Historiâ facti Butleri, Gordon, Lesly et Aliorum. *Moguntiae*, Anno Christi 1639.
Account of Walter, Count Leslie, in Latin, by the Rev. Paul Tafferner.
Reciant's Book of Turkish Fashions. *Vienna*, 1672.
John Burbury's Account of Lord Henry Arundel's Journey to Constantinople with Count Leslie.
A Relation or Diary of the Siege of Vienna. Written by John Peter a Valcaren, Judge-Advocate of the Imperial Army. *London*, 1684.
Baden Historical Lexicon.
Iselin's Historical Lexicon. *Basle*, 1743.
Almanach de Gotha.
Austrian Army List. *Vienna*, 1841.

AUTHORITIES.

Rymer's Fœdera.
Andrew Wyntoun's Chronicles.
Hollinshead's Chronicles.
Pinkerton's Chronicles.
Fordoun's Chronicles.
Pitscotti's Chronicles.
Camden's Britannia.
Maitland's Historical Tales of Scotland.
Irvine's Lives of Scotch Writers. *Edinburgh,* 1824.
Spalding Club Publications.

LIST of GENTLEMEN and LADIES who have afforded Authentic Information to Colonel CHARLES LESLIE, K.H., of Balquhain, for the "HISTORICAL RECORDS OF THE FAMILY OF LESLIE." CONTRIBUTORS.

1. Mons. TEULET, Director of the Archives du Royaume, Soubise Palace, Paris, 1845.
2. Mr. ALEXANDER DEUCHAR, Genealogist, Edinburgh.
3. Mr. ALEXANDER MACDONALD, Register House, Edinburgh.
4. Dr. JOSEPH ROBERTSON, Register House, Edinburgh.
5. COSMO INNES, Esq., Register House, Edinburgh.
6. JOHN STUART, Esq., LL.D., Register House, Edinburgh.
7. ROBERT CHAMBERS, Esq., Edinburgh.
8. HUGH CRICHTON, Esq., W.S., Edinburgh.
9. ALEXANDER SINCLAIR, Esq., Edinburgh.
10. Sir WILLIAM BETHAM, Ulster King-at-Arms, Dublin.
11. Mr. THOMAS HORSBURGH, Town-Clerk, Cupar.
12. The Right Rev. Dr. KYLE
13. Sir CHARLES TREVELYAN.
14. Sir ROBERT ABERCROMBIE, Bart. of Birkenbog.
15. Colonel TYTLER.
16. JAMES TYTLER, Esq. of Woodhouselee.
17. The Rev. HAMILTON GREY, Bolsover.
18. FRANCIS SEYMOUR LESLIE, Esq., Home Office, London.
19. Lord MURRAY.

20. Mr. JOHN GRANT LESLIE, Sheriff-clerk-depute, Aberdeen.
21. EDWARD TUDOR SCARGILL, Esq., London.
22. Mr. LAING, Librarian to the Writers to the Signet, Edinburgh.

1. The Countess of ROTHES.
2. LOUISA, Countess of ROTHES.
3. The Countess DE SALIS.
4. Lady GORDON HALIBURTON.
5. Mrs. GURDON, Daughter of Col. Charles Powell Leslie of Glasslough.
6. Miss AGNES STRICKLAND.

CONTENTS OF VOL. I.

CHAPTER I.
                                                           PAGES
Dynasta de Leslie 1-36
Notes to Chapter I. 37-44

CHAPTER II.
Leslies, Barons of Leslie 45-64

CHAPTER III.
Leslies, Earls and Countesses of Ross . . . 65-93

CHAPTER IV.
The Garioch; Parish of Chapel of Garioch; Balquhain Castle; Fetternear; Parish of Leslie; Leslie Castle; Rothes 94-143

APPENDIX.

1. Charter of lands of Leslie, etc., granted to Malcolm the son of Bertolf, by David, Earl of Huntingdon—1171-1199 147
2. Charter to Abbey of Arbroath, by David, Earl of Huntingdon, witnessed by Malcolm*. . . 148
3. Charter of Lesselyn, etc., to Norman, the son of Malcolm, by John, Earl of Huntingdon—1219-1237 148-149
4. Charter for erection of St. Peter's Hospital near Aberdeen, by Bishop Kinninmount, witnessed by Norman, the Constable of Inverurie—1165-1169   149-150

		PAGES
5.	Charter of Foundation of Lindores Church and Abbey, witnessed by Norman, the Constable of Inverurie—1202-1206	150-152
6.	Charter of Leslie in Free Forest, granted by Alexander II. to Norino, son of Norman—1248	152
7.	Discharge for £200 sterling by Sir Andrew de Leslie, the eighth Lord—1376 . . .	153
8.	Charter by Robert III., in favour of Norman de Leslie and Sir George Leslie of Rothes—1390	153-154
9.	Charter by Sir Andrew de Leslie, eighth Lord, to David de Abercrombie and his wife Margaret de Leslie—1391	155
10.	Charter by Robert III., confirming a charter by Norman de Leslie, knight, to Sir John Ramsay of Culathy—1392	156-157
11.	Resignation of Brawkawche, etc., by George Leslie, second Baron of that Ilk, in favour of Patrick Gordon of Methlic—1490-1500 . . .	157-158
12.	Charter of half the lands of Edingarioch and Chapeltown, granted by James IV. to George Leslie, second Baron, and his wife—1497 .	158-159
13.	Confirmation by James IV. of a part of Chapeltown in Garioch, to George Leslie, the second Baron, and his wife—1505	159
14.	Charter to Chaplains of Choir of Aberdeen Church, by Alexander Leslie, fourth Baron of that Ilk, and his wife—1527	160
15.	Instrument to Margaret Leslie, of John Leslie or Master T. Mortymar as a fit husband for her—1544	161
16.	Lease for nineteen years of teind-sheaves of Leslie, etc., by the Abbot of Lindores, to John Leslie, fifth of that Ilk, and his wife—1546 . .	162-163

17. Feu-charter of Kirkland and Glebe of Vicarage of
Leslie, to John Leslie, fifth of that Ilk, by Sir
Thomas Raith, Vicar of the Parish—1561 . 163-164

18. Lease for twice nineteen years of the Teinds of
Mains of Leslie, etc., by John Leslie, Vicar of
Pramott, to John Leslie, fifth of that Ilk—1579 165-166

19. The Earldom of Ross 166-176

20. Charter of Tiry in Buchan, etc., by Walter Leslie,
Earl of Ross, to Eufemia de Sancto Claro—
1367 176

21. Charter of Aberchirder, etc., by David II., to Sir
Walter de Leslie and his wife—1369 . . 177

22. Charter of Aberchirder and Kincardine, to Sir
Walter de Leslie, by David II., 1369 . . 178

23. Charter by David II., of Earldom of Ross, Lordship of Sky, etc., to William, Earl of Ross, etc.—
1370 179-180

24. Complaint to Robert II., by William, Earl of Ross,
about the Earl's lands in Buchan, etc., having
been given to Sir Walter Leslie, and how the
said Sir Walter married the Earl's daughter
against her father's will—1371 . . . 181-183

25. Charter by Walter Leslie, Earl of Ross, and his
wife, to Sir Alexander Fraser and his wife, of
the lands of Auchinschogle, etc.—1375 . . 183-184

26. Charter by Euphamia, Countess of Ross, confirming grant made to Andrew Mercer of the lands
of Faythley, etc.—1382 185-186

27. Judgment pronounced by the Bishops of Moray
and Ross on the difference between Alexander
Stewart, Earl of Buchan, and his wife, Eufamia,
Countess of Ross—1389 . . . 187-188

Pedigree
OF THE
Original Family of Leslie.

1. Bartholomew, came to Scotland 1067, *d.* 1121.
2. Malcolm, got charter 1165.
3. Norman, got charter 1224.
4. Norino, got charter 1248.
5. Sir Norman, got Fythkill 1282.
6. Sir Andrew, *m.* Mary Abernethy; got Ballinbreich and Cairney 1314.

7. Sir Andrew, 1325-1353.
8. Sir Andrew, 1353-1398.

Norman *d.* 1391.

9. David de Leslie, *d.* 1439.

Margaret, *m.* to Alexander Leslie, and carried on the family of Leslie, Barons of that Ilk.

Walter, Earl of Ross, *m.* Euphemia, Countess of Ross, 1365.

Alexander, Earl of Ross, *d.* before 1411.

Euphemia, *d.* S. P. 1415.

—— Leslie.

Sir George Leslie of Rothes, *d.* 1411.

Sir Norman Leslie of Rothes succeeded to Ballinbreich, &c., 1439.

George, created Earl of Rothes.

George Leslie got the Barony of Balquhain 1340.

Hamelin, Second Baron of Balquhain.

Sir Andrew, Third Baron of Balquhain.

Sir William, Fourth Baron of Balquhain, ancestor of the Leslies of Kincraigie, Wardis, New Leslie, Pitcaple, and Iden.

CHAPTER I.

Dynasta de Leslie.

1. BARTHOLOMEW,

FOUNDER OF THE FAMILY OF LESLIE.

Bartholomew Founder.

ACCORDING both to tradition and to Bishop Leslie in his *De Rebus Gestis Scotorum*, lib. vi. p. 200, Romæ, 1578, Bartholomew or Bartholf, a noble Hungarian, the founder of the family of Leslie, came to Scotland in the train of Margaret, afterwards the queen of Malcolm Canmore, in 1067.

1067.

Edgar Etheling, the brother of this noble lady, was the grandson of Edmund Ironside, King of England, being the son of Prince Edward, surnamed the Outlaw, by Agatha his wife, daughter of Henry II., Emperor of Germany. Edgar thus concentrated in his own person all the Anglo-Saxon claims to the crown of England. Excluded from his just right of succession, first by the usurpation of Harold, and afterwards by the conquest of William the Norman, in order to promote the happiness of the people, and, in accordance with the advice of his uncles, Edwin and Morcar, he abandoned his claims, and swore fealty to the conqueror at Berkhamstead 25th

CHAP. I.
Bartholomew Founder.
1066.

December 1066. William, anxious from motives of policy to conciliate the affections of his Anglo-Saxon subjects, and more especially to honour one whose claims might be dangerous to his power, took Edgar into great favour, and bestowed upon him an earldom with large possessions.

After completing his conquest, William found it necessary to revisit his native duchy. He returned to Normandy in 1067, in the spring of the year, and, partly to deprive insurrection in England of any chance of success, and partly to impress on his Norman subjects the due value of his success, he carried Edgar Etheling along with him to grace the pageantry of his triumph.

The English, however, did take advantage of William's absence to make some effort for freedom, and insurrections were made in various parts of the country. The suspicions of William, caused by these outbreaks, though veiled under the mask of apparent friendship, did not escape the notice of Edgar, who accordingly determined to flee the dangerous precincts of the Norman Court. He took shipping, in company with his mother Agatha, and his sisters Margaret and Christina, with the intention of returning to Hungary, the land of their birth. Stress of weather, however, drove their vessel into the Firth of Forth at St. Margaret's Hope, Queensferry, where they were graciously received by Malcolm, King of Scotland, who was then residing in his palace at Dunfermline. This prince, struck with the beauty and won by the accomplishments of the Princess Margaret, offered her his hand, and the offer was accepted. Having thus become the consort of an unpolished king, and the queen of a rude and barbarous people, Margaret so gained the esteem and affection of her husband, and used her power so well for the benefit of her adopted people, that they in their gratitude invested her with the qualities of a saint, by which appellation the good queen is still known in Scottish history; and in memory of her welcome arrival in the country, the place where she first set foot on Scottish ground was named St. Margaret's Hope, and to this day it retains the name of Queensferry.

Bartholomew Founder.

Among the noblemen who accompanied the Princess Agatha from Germany, and who, sharing her unsettled fortunes, faithfully attended her and her children until their arrival in Scotland, was a Hungarian, named Bartolf or Bartholomew, who was descended from an ancient and noble family in Hungary. Bartholomew was a man of acute genius and strong mind, very valiant, and possessed of great bodily strength—qualities which are always valuable in a rude age, and which recommended him to the favour of King Malcolm, who appointed him Governor of the Castle of Edinburgh, honoured him with the dignity of knighthood, and bestowed on him large grants of land in Fife, Angus, the Mearns, and Aberdeenshire. The cir-

Bartholomew Founder.

cumstances of this grant are recorded in the following legend:—

Commencing his journey on horseback at Dunfermline, and proceeding northward, Bartholomew was promised by the king in hereditary right, all the land for a mile round any point where he should find it necessary to alight for the purpose of baiting or feeding his horse. First, he alighted at Fechil, now called Leslie, in Fife; next at Innerlessad, in Angus; the third time at Feskie, or Eskie, in the Mearns; the fourth time at Cushnie, in Mar. His horse at last failed him at the place called Leslie in the Garioch. On his return to court, the king asked him where he had left his horse, and he replied, as some say—

"At the lesse ley beside the mair."

or, as others give it—

"Between a lesse ley and a mair,"
My horse it tyrd and stopped there."

The king, finding, it is said, that the place suited well with his surname, answered in the same metrical style—

"Lord Lesley shalt thou be,
And thy heirs after thee."

and he honourably fulfilled the terms of his promise. Traditions generally arise in later times to account for prior facts, and though they may alter the accessories of events, yet the foundation on which they rest is not unfrequently found to be according to truth. All the places mentioned in this tradition did, at later dates, belong to the family of Leslie, as will be shown in the proper place. It is also beyond doubt that Bartholomew did obtain from the king a grant of the lands of Lesselyn in the Garioch, which long remained the patrimony of his successors. Three charters, now in possession of the Countess of Rothes, granted to Malcolm son of Bartolf, Norman son of Malcolm, and Norino son of Norman, place this fact beyond the reach of cavil.

The parish of Leslie, in the district of the Garioch and county of Aberdeen, was thus the earliest possession of the family of Leslie in Scotland. From it unquestionably the family derived its patronymic. As is the case of most of the old Scottish families, so here the family estate gave the cognomen to the family, and, as will be shown afterwards, not until the fifth generation did this family bend to the custom then becoming general, of assuming a surname, a fact which would seem to clear up all doubt that may exist as to the origin of the name of Leslie.

The present castle of Leslie, built, without doubt, on the site of an earlier stronghold, is situated on the banks of the river Gaudy, which runs at the back, or north-west side of the celebrated hill of Bennachie. In later times so numerously did the Leslies cluster round this their ancestral domain that the circumstance is commemorated in a beautiful old song—

CHAP. I.
Bartholomew Founder.

See App. Nos. I. II. III.

CHAP. I.

Bartholomew Founder.

> "Thick sit the Leslies on Gaudy side,
> On Gaudy side, on Gaudy side,
> At the back of Bennachie."

Robert Verstigan relates, in reference to Bartholomew, that a duel took place between a Scottish nobleman of the name of Leslie and a foreign knight, in which the Scottish champion was victorious, in memory of which the following verses existed in Scotland :—

> "Between the Lesseley and the mair,
> He slew the knight, and left him there."

This story, however, seems to refer to Bartholomew's descendant, Sir Walter Leslie, the famous Earl of Ross.

It may be proper here to give a description of the family arms. They are a field argent, traversed with a belt or girdle azure, in which are three buckles gules, supported on the dexter and sinister side by two griffins proper. The crest is a demi-griffin proper, having a scroll with the motto "Grip Fast." The origin of these arms is thus related by tradition :—

Bartholomew held the office of Lord Chamberlain to the Queen, and had the honour, according to the primitive fashion of those times, of carrying the Queen on his own horse when she travelled. For ease a pad behind the Chamberlain was provided for the Queen, and, for safety, a belt buckled round his waist, supplied her with a stay in case of danger or uneasy motion. On one occasion, when both thus mounted were crossing a river, the Queen nearly fell from the horse. On this the Chamberlain in great anxiety, called out, "Grip fast," to which the Queen, doubtful of the strength of the buckle, replied, "Gin the buckle bide." To obviate the danger of the buckle giving way in future, two more buckles were forthwith added to the belt. And, in commemoration of the event, says the legend, Bartholomew got the above device for his family arms.

Bartholomew, the founder of the family of Leslie in Scotland, married, according to some authorities, one of the ladies of honour to Queen Margaret. According to others, King Malcolm gave him to wife one of his own sisters, and this account is fortified by the best authorities. The Rev. William Betham, in his *Genealogical Tables*, published in 1795, states that Bartholomew married a sister of King Malcolm Canmore; and in the *Genealogical Tree of the Royal Family of Scotland*, published 3d March 1792, by John Brown, Genealogist in Scotland to the Prince of Wales, and approved by the Lyon Office, we find it stated that, "Beatrix, daughter of King Duncan, and sister of Malcolm III. or Canmore, married Bartholomew, of whom all the Leslies in Scotland are descended."

From this marriage have sprung the many noble, knightly, and gentle houses of the illustrious name of Leslie. Many of these have risen to great splendour and rank, some deriving their dignities and wealth from the well-merited gratitude of royalty, for distinguished services, and others from intermarriage with the noblest houses in this and in other countries. In most parts of the Continent, indeed, cadets of this ancient stock have been found enjoying the highest reputation, supporting the greatest dignities, and discharging the most distinguished and honourable offices. No Scottish surname has been more widely conspicuous abroad. And in Germany, Sweden, Russia, Poland, France, and Ireland, the name of Leslie is known almost as familiarly as the names of the great native houses of those countries.

The family of Leslie was also distinguished as among the first to introduce a practical and improved system of agriculture. The district now inhabited by a united people speaking the same tongue, was, at that remote period, occupied by discordant tribes of Scots, Saxons, Danes, Normans, and Flemings, each using their own language, and each following their peculiar customs. Learned antiquarians inform us that it was chiefly owing to the settlement of the house of Leslie that these various races were gradually rendered more civilised, and became incorporated into one homogeneous body, and that much of the great distinctive character of industry, perseverance, and agricultural skill, for which the people of the Garioch are now, as they had been early, celebrated, is to be ascribed to Bartholomew and his successors, the chiefs of the House of Leslie.

Bartholomew, the founder of the family of Leslie, died at an advanced age, about 1121, and was succeeded by his son Malcolm.

CHAP. I.
Bartholomew Founder.
1121.

II. MALCOLM.

Malcolm.

MALCOLM, son of Bartholomew, succeeded his father as head of the house of Leslie about 1121, as is authenticated by a charter still extant.

1121.

Imitating his father, Bartholomew, in bravery and other noble qualities, Malcolm was accounted by King William the Lion worthy of the honour of knighthood.

The lordship of the Garioch in Aberdeenshire, which had been erected into a regality, was at this time held by the King's brother, David, Earl of Huntingdon. From this prince, Malcolm received a charter of confirmation of his lands of Lessel, Hachennegart, and Mache, to be held by the tenure of one knight's service. In this charter he is styled Malcolm, the son of Bertolf. This is the most ancient charter of any lands in Aberdeenshire, except church-lands, and must have been granted after 1165, when William the Lion succeeded to the throne of Scotland, and before 1197, when Matthew, Bishop of Aberdeen, who is a witness to the charter, died.

See App. No. 1.

As Lord of the Garioch, David, Earl of

Huntingdon, possessed a castle or stronghold at Inverurie, the capital of the district, commanding the passage of the river Don, which separates the district of the Garioch from that of Mar. The office of constable of this castle Earl David conferred upon Malcolm, as appears from a charter granted by the Earl to the abbey of Lindores.*

In these times the Constable of Inverurie was a person of note, and for three generations at least this was the only style by which the progenitors of the noble house of Leslie were distinguished. Indeed the " Constable of Inverurie " is a frequent witness to the charters of Earl David and of his successors in the lordship of the Garioch, John, Earl of Huntington, and Isabella Bruce, his sister, between 1147 and 1219.†

Malcolm, the son of Bartolf, is a witness to a charter granted by David, Earl of Huntingdon, Lord of the Garioch, to the abbey of Arbroath.

No record gives us the name of Malcolm's wife, but by her it is certain that he had two sons—

    I. NORMAN, his successor ;
    II. MALCOLM, who was killed in the Crusades.

Malcolm, the son of Bartholomew, died about 1176, and was succeeded by his son Norman.

---

* See Balfour of Denmyln's *Collections*, p. 22, No. 40. MSS. Advocates' Library, Edinburgh.
† *Book of Bonaccord*, p. 375.

III. NORMAN.

NORMAN, the son of Malcolm, succeeded his father about 1176.

About the year 1224 Norman obtained a charter confirming to him, as Norman the son of Malcolm, the lands of Lesselyn, Achnagart, and Mile, and their pertinents, with the exception of the church of Lesselyn, which the said Norman had previously granted to the abbey and monks of Lindores. By this charter Norman also received a grant, for the first time that the family held them, of the lands of Caskyben, now called Keith Hall.

Norman appears to have succeeded his father Malcolm in his office of Constable of Inverurie. Under this title he is named as a witness in a deed by which David, Earl of Huntingdon, renounced, in favour of the Earl of Mar, all claim to a serf called Gillecriste MacGillekuncongal, and his four sons, the two Gillecristes, and Gillenem, and Gillemartin.*

Norman, the Constable of Inverurie, also appears as a witness to a charter granted in the reign of William the Lion, by Matthew Kinninmount, Bishop of Aberdeen from 1165 to 1197,

---

* See *Illustrations of Scottish History*, pp. 23, 24, Glasgow, 1834 ; and *Antiquities of the Shires of Aberdeen and Banff*, vol. iii. p. 402.

for the erection of St. Peter's Hospital in the Spittal, near Aberdeen.

Norman, the son of Malcolm, and Constable of Inverurie, is also one of the witnesses to the charter of foundation granted to the Church and abbey of Lindores, by David, Earl of Huntingdon, between 1202 and 1206.

Norman, the son of Malcolm, married a daughter of Stuart, Earl of Lorn, by whom he had—

 I. Norino, his successor;
 II. Leonard, who, some say, succeeded his brother Norino;
 III. Bartholomew, who died young.

It has not been ascertained when Norman, the third possessor of the lands of Leslie, died. He was succeeded by his son Norino.

IV. NORINO.

Norino, the son of Norman by his wife, a daughter of Stuart, Earl of Lorn, succeeded his father as fourth possessor of the lands of Leslie.

This is proved by a charter granted in 1248 by King Alexander II. at the instance of Isobel Bruce and Robert Bruce her son; Isobel Bruce, on the death of John, Earl of Huntingdon, without issue in 1237, having succeeded to the lordship of the Garioch in right of her father, David, Earl of Huntingdon. By this charter, in which he is styled the son of Norman, Norino received his lands of Leslie in free forest, and in it he is likewise styled "The Constable," *i.e.* of Inverurie. Hence this office of Constable of Inverurie would now seem to have been confirmed in hereditary succession in the family.

Norino is a frequent witness to the charters of his liege lady, Isobel de Bruce, of whose court indeed he appears to have been a principal officer. We find also that "Norino, the son of Norman," was witness to a charter granted by Fergus, Earl of Buchan, to John, the son of Uthred.*

These facts indisputably prove that NORINO was the name of the successor of Norman, the third possessor of the lands of Leslie, although by some authors he has been called ALFORNUS, and by others LEONARD.

It is probable that Norino had a brother Leonard, whom the author of the *Laurus Leslæana*, has, by mistake, to the exclusion of Norino, placed in the position of the head of the family, and of whom he gives the following account:—

"Leonard was honoured with the dignity of knighthood. He was a man of great courage, and was held in great estimation by the kings both of Scotland and of England. Clarcadus makes mention of him in his work. He married Catherine Mure, heiress of Tasseis in Fife, which

---

* See original Charter in Charter-room at Pitfour, and Charter published in *Collections for Shires of Aberdeen and Banff*, p. 409, Spalding Club.

property was added to the family possessions. By her he had—

    I. NORMAN, who succeeded;
    II. LEONARD, who went to the wars abroad;
    III. WILLIAM, Abbot of Cupar.

In the above account LEONARD is evidently a mistake for NORINO. It is also doubtful whether the author of the *Laurus Leslæana* has given the proper name of the heiress of Taces. It is certain that this property of Taces came about this time into the possession of the family of Leslie by marriage. In the charter-room of the Earls of Rothes there is a charter granted by Malcolm, Earl of Fife, to Alexander de Blar, of the lands of Thases (Taces), Kinteaces, and Ballindurth, to be holden of the said Earl and his heirs by the tenure of one knight's service. This charter has the Earl's seal appended, and bears no date, but it must have been granted before the year 1250. From this charter it would appear that Blar, not Mure, must have been the name of the heiress who shortly afterwards brought the property of Taces into the possession of the family of Leslie.

While it is doubtful whether Norino had a brother named Leonard, it is certain that the succession of the family was carried on by Norman, the son either of Norino or of Leonard, and who was the first of the family who signed the surname "de Leslie."

V. SIR NORMAN DE LESLIE,

DOMINUS DE LESLIE, OR DOMINUS EJUSDEM.

NORMAN succeeded Norino as fifth possessor of the lands of Leslie. It appears that he was the first of the family who was distinguished by the surname of Leslie; for while his predecessors had only been known either by their patronymics, or by the offices which they held, such as that of Constable of Inverurie, he is styled in all public documents "Norman de Lesley, dominus de Lesley," or "dominus ejusdem."

Norman de Leslie also received the honour of knighthood. The *Laurus Leslæana* states that Sir Norman de Leslie received from King Alexander III. the gift of the forest of Leslie in the king's forest, 4th December 1282. Douglas states that he also got Fytekill, now called Leslie in Fife, from the same king.

It is recorded in the "Ragman's Roll" that King Edward I. of England arrived at Aberdeen on Saturday, 14th July 1296, and that on the morrow, the 15th, there swore fealty to him at that place—Sir Norman de Lesselyn, Chevalier, Sir Alexander Lamberton, and others; and that on Monday the 16th, and following days, Sir Gilbert de la Haye, Sir Hugh de la Haye, Sir William Innes, and on the 19th, Henry, Bishop of Aberdeen, performed the like homage to the English king.

Sir Norman de Leslie was also one of the magnates of Scotland, who, 12th July 1296, in compliance with the wishes of the oppressor of their country, renounced the old Scottish league with France.*

Sir Norman de Leslie was one of those summoned by King Edward to attend the parliament held at Berwick, 24th August 1296.†

Probably it was for compliances such as these, of which it would be difficult to fix the adequate blame, but which no patriot can consider excusable, that King Edward appointed Sir Norman de Leslie sheriff of his native country of Aberdeen in 1305.

Sir Norman de Leslie, however, availed himself of an early opportunity of returning to his rightful allegiance. He sat in the parliament which was held by King Robert Bruce at Cambuskenneth, 6th December 1314, and signed the decree of forfeiture issued by that parliament against all those who refused to return to their allegiance after the battle of Bannockburn.‡

The *Laurus Leslæana* does not mention the name of the wife of Sir Norman de Leslie. In Douglas's *Peerage*, however, it is stated that he married Elizabeth Leith, heiress of Edengarioch,

---

* See *Ragman's Roll*, pp. 92, 93, 100.
† *Ibid.* p. 142.
‡ See *Appendix to the Lord of the Isles*, p. 347, note B. 2.

THE FAMILY OF LESLIE.

in Aberdeenshire; while Shaw, in his *History of Moray*, on the other hand, says that "in the end of the reign of Alexander III. (about 1280) Norman Lesley, son of Lesley in the Garioch, married the daughter and heiress, it is said, of Watson of Rothes." Whichever of these accounts be correct, it is at all events certain that Sir Norman de Leslie had a son—

    ANDREW, his successor.

Besides this son, however, the *Laurus Leslæana* states that Sir Norman had another—Walter, Earl of Ross; but, as will be shown hereafter, in treating of that Earl, this statement is inconsistent with correct chronology.

In Douglas's *Peerage* it is stated that Sir Norman had also two daughters—

    I. MARGARET, married to Sir John Innes of Innes;
    II. ANN, married to Sir Alexander Dunbar of Westfield.

This statement appears to be correct, although the *Laurus Leslæana* describes these ladies as daughters of Sir Norman's son Andrew.

Sir Norman de Leslie is a contracting party to the marriage-agreement of his son Sir Andrew de Leslie with Mary Abernethy, in 1313.

Sir Norman de Leslie died before 1320, in which year the name of his son, Sir Andrew de Leslie, Dominus Ejusdem, appears in the list of the greater barons of Scotland, who in that year addressed their memorable letter of remonstrance to the Pope.

VI. SIR ANDREW DE LESLIE,

DOMINUS EJUSDEM.

Sir Andrew de Leslie succeeded his father, Sir Norman de Leslie, as VI. Dominus Ejusdem before 1320.

Sir Andrew de Leslie married Mary Abernethy, one of the daughters and co-heiresses of Sir Alexander Abernethy, Lord of Abernethy, who died about 1312.

With his wife, Mary Abernethy, Sir Andrew de Leslie got the baronies of Ballinbreich in Fifeshire, Cairney in Forfar, and various other lands, and, it is said, Rothes in Elgin, but of this no record has been found. He got charters of Ballinbreich and Cairney from King Robert I., and quartered the arms of Abernethy with his own.

This marriage between Sir Andrew de Leslie and Mary Abernethy is documented by an indenture between Andrew de Leslie, son and heir of Norman de Leslie, Chevalier, with the consent of Mary, his wife, as heiress of the deceased Sir Alexander Abernethy, on the one part, and Sir William Lindsay, Rector of Ayr, and Chamberlain of Scotland from 1312 to 1322, on the other part, whereby the said Sir Andrew obliges himself to infeft Sir William Lindsay in twenty-four merks land in the tenement of Cairney, to be held of the granter, dated 25th December 1316.*

By his marriage with Mary Abernethy, Sir Andrew de Leslie had the following issue:—

  I. ANDREW, who succeeded as VII. Dominus Ejusdem.
  II. NORMAN, of whom presently.
  III.   LESLIE, ancestor of the Earls of Rothes, of whom hereafter under "Records of the Earls of Rothes."
  IV. WALTER, Earl of Ross, of whom hereafter.
  V. GEORGE, 1st Baron of Balquhain, of whom hereafter.†

Norman de Leslie, Sir Andrew's second son, was a man of great abilities, and was much employed in the public transactions of his time. During the reign of King David II. we find him mentioned in the following extracts from public documents:—

"Et nihil hic per firmam Baronie de Comnay (Kemnay) que est in manu magistri Normani de Lesley ex concessione Roberti senescalli Scotiae locum tenentis Domini Regis ratione warde super quo consulatur Rex."

"Ex comp. Domini Alexandri Fraser, vicecomitis de Aberdeen" (1348).

Norman de Leslie, Domicellus de Scotia (and not Dominus Ejusdem), is a witness to the com-

---

* See *Chartulary of Melrose*, vol. i. p. 348; Lindsay's *Lives of the Lindsays*, vol. i. p. 61, note; and Douglas's *Peerage*, vol. ii. p. 424. *See* also Note A—Lordship of Abernethy.

† *See* Note B—*Laurus Leslæana*, account of Sir Andrew de Leslie's marriage and issue.

mission issued by the Steward of Scotland, 10th May 1356, to treat for the liberation of David II. when at Durham.

Norman Lesselyn et Wauter, son frere, Esquires d'Ecosse, had a safe conduct to pass through England on their way to Prussia, 20th August 1356.*

Norman de Lesseley had a safe conduct into England, 11th May 1358, and again, 24th March 1359, as one of the Scottish commissioners appointed to treat with the English.†

Norman de Leslie was, in 1358, sent along with Sir Robert Erskine as ambassador to Rome, to solicit the Pope for a grant of the tenth part of the ecclesiastical revenues of Scotland, towards payment of the ransom of David II., which they obtained for three years.

It appears by the following extract that Norman de Leslie was Deputy-Chamberlain to Thomas Earl of Angus, Chamberlain of Scotland:—

"Et lxvi. vi. viij. (£66 : 6 : 8) liberat Normano de Lesley, tunc locum tenenti camerarii Scocie confident receptionem super compotum de quibus respondebit" (1358).

In the accounts of customs and money paid by Aberdeen to government from 1328 to 1399, we find the following charge:—"Compotum Normani de Lesley, locum tenentis Thome Comitis de Angus dudum camerarii Scocie reddit apud

---

* *Rotuli Scotiæ*, vol. i. p. 797.   † *Ibid.* pp. 823, 837.

Dunde IXmo die Aprilis, Anno Domini Millio ccc q'nqᵃgᶜnono"* (1359).

Norman de Leslie is styled by King David II. "Armiger noster," *i.e.* King's armour-bearer, in a commission dated at Edinburgh, 10th May 1359, whereby Sir Robert Erskine, Norman de Leslie, and Sir John Grant were constituted plenipotentiaries to treat with Charles, the Dauphin of France, then Regent of France, to renew the old league thitherto inviolably observed between the two kingdoms, in which mission they succeeded.†

Norman de Leslie had a safe conduct to go into England as one of the ambassadors sent to treat in the affairs of King David II., then a prisoner in England, 15th April 1362; and again, 14th March 1363, for himself and eight esquires.‡

Norman de Leslie was a member of the assembly held at Inchmurdoch, 14th May 1363, when the Steward of Scotland entered into an obligation to adhere to King David II.

It appears by Robertson's *Index of Missing Charters of David II.*, No. 46, that Norman de Leslie received "ane pension enduring the ward of Balenbreich," between 1330 and 1370.

Norman de Leslie married Margaret Lamber-

---

* *See* Kennedy's *Annals of Aberdeen*, vol. i. p. 41.
† *See* Abercromby's *History*, vol. ii. p. 124.
‡ *Rotuli Scotiæ*, vol. i. pp. 862, 872.

ton, granddaughter and heiress of Alexander de Lamberton, and with her he got a good fortune. The marriage is documented by a charter granted by Margaret de Leslie, relict of the deceased Norman de Leslie, Knight, to her cousin, William Cuppyld, and Norman his son, of all and whole of the lands which formerly belonged to Alexander de Lamberton, her grandfather—namely, Lumlathyn and Cragoe in the county of Forfar, and Asdory in the county of Fife. This charter is witnessed by "nobili viro Domino Waltero de Lesley," who is styled her brother (in law). "Nobili Domina Margarita Comitissa Angusie, nobili viro Domino Alexandro de Lindsey, milite, Laurentio Archidiacono Brehinensi, et multis aliis," and was confirmed by David II., an. reg. 37, 11th February—*i. e.* A.D. 1366.*

This proves that Norman de Leslie died before 11th February 1366. And he does not seem to have had any children by his marriage with Margaret Lamberton, since, according to the above charter, that lady's property, apparently in default of direct heirs, passed into the possession of her cousin, William Cuppyld. †

Sir Andrew de Leslie, VI. Dominus Ejusdem, was one of the great barons or Magnates Scotiæ, who signed the memorable letter, dated at Arbrothawik, 6th April 1320, addressed to Pope John

---

* See Robertson's *Index of Missing Charters of David II.*, No. 251.
† See Note C—Errors regarding Norman de Leslie.

XXII., asserting the independence of Scotland in opposition to the Pope's orders to excommunicate King Robert Bruce and his followers on every Sunday and festival throughout the year.*

Sir Andrew de Leslie, VI. Dominus Ejusdem, died before 1325, as in that year Mary Abernethy, his wife, after her husband's death, married Sir David Lindsay of Crawford, ancestor of the Earls of Crawford, as is proved by a dispensation from Pope John XXII., which dispensation was found by Andrew Stewart in the Vatican.†

By Sir David Lindsay, Mary Abernethy had issue—

> I. Sir JAMES LINDSAY, Sir David's successor, who married Lady Egidia Stewart in 1346, and died after 1357, leaving a son—
>> I. Sir JAMES, who married Christian Keith, and died 1397.
>
> II. Sir ALEXANDER LINDSAY of Glenesk, who married Catherine Stirling, and died 1382, leaving a son—
>> I. Sir DAVID, created Earl of Crawford, 1398.
>
> III. Sir WILLIAM LINDSAY, of the Byres, who married Catherine Muir, and died after 1375, leaving a son, Sir William, who carried on that branch of the family.

Walter Leslie, Earl of Ross, in several charters, styles Sir Alexander Lindsay of Glenesk and Sir William Lindsay of Byres "carissimi fratres," they being his uterine brothers.

---

* *See* Note D—Letter addressed by Barons to Pope John XXII.
† *See* Andrew Stewart's *History of the Stewarts*, p. 446.

VII. SIR ANDREW DE LESLIE,

DOMINUS EJUSDEM.

Sir Andrew de Leslie, eldest son of Sir Andrew de Leslie, by his wife Mary Abernethy, succeeded his father as VII. Dominus Ejusdem, before 1325, and appears to have died before 1353, leaving issue—

> I. Andrew his successor;
> II. Margaret married to David de Abercrombie, who in 1391 got a charter of Aquhortis, Blairdaff, etc., from Sir Andrew de Leslie, VIII. Dominus Ejusdem, his brother-in-law.

VIII. SIR ANDREW DE LESLIE,

DOMINUS EJUSDEM.

Sir Andrew de Leslie, son of Sir Andrew de Leslie, VII. Dominus Ejusdem, succeeded his father as VIII. Dominus Ejusdem before 1353.

There is a charter in the possession of the Earl of Strathmore, by which Andrew de Leslie, Dominus Ejusdem, confirms a charter from Walter de Leslie, Dominus de Philorth, of all the lands which the said Walter had in territorio de Monergood, to John Lyon de Terteviot. In this charter Sir Andrew de Leslie calls Sir Walter de Leslie his uncle—viz., "Sciatis nos vidisse cartam dilecti patrui nostri Walteri de Lesley de Philorth, &c."

There is no date in this charter of confirmation, but it must have been granted between 1365, the year in which Sir Walter de Leslie married Euphemia, daughter of the Earl of Ross, and assumed the title of Lord of Philorth, and the year 1372, when he became Earl of Ross in right of his wife, on the death of William, Earl of Ross, his father-in-law.

In a charter by Sir Andrew de Leslie of that Ilk, in favour of Sir Hugh Barclay of Kilnaim, Sir Andrew gives Sir Hugh 24 merks yearly out of his barony of Ballinbreich. The witnesses are, Alexander and Patrick, Bishops of Aberdeen and Brechin; Roger and Patrick, Abbots of Lindores and Balmerino; "Waltero de Lesley, Domino de Ross, patruo suo;" James de Lindsay; William de Ramsay de Colthithie; John de Kinloch; and many others.

This charter must have been granted between 1373, when Sir Walter de Leslie became Earl of Ross, and 1381, when Alexander Kininmund, Bishop of Aberdeen, died.

Sir Andrew de Leslie granted a charter of the lands of Culmelly and Auld Culmelly, in the barony of Cushney in Aberdeenshire, to Bernard de Kergyle, which charter was confirmed by King Robert II., 8th January 1373.*

* See *Registrum Magni Sigili*, p. 100, No. 26.

In the charter-room of the Earl of Errol there is a discharge by Sir Andrew de Leslie, Dominus Ejusdem, to Thomas de Haia, Lord of Errol, for £200, good and lawful sterling, which the said Thomas stood bound to pay to the said Andrew, by reason of a contract of marriage between the said Sir Andrew's son and Lord Errol's daughter. The discharge is dated at Dundee, 12th July 1376.

In a charter to his uncle Walter, Earl of Ross, Sir Andrew de Leslie, VIII. Dominus Ejusdem, calls Sir James de Lindsay, Dominus de Crawford, consanguineus suus (his cousin), and Sir Alexander Lindsay of Glenesk, patruus suus (his uncle), they being thus related through Mary Abernethy, the grandmother of Sir Andrew de Leslie and Sir James de Lindsay, and the mother of Sir Alexander Lindsay of Glenesk.

Sir Andrew de Leslie, Dominus Ejusdem, confirmed a charter granted by Andrew de Garvyack, Dominus de Caskyben, anent the devolution of his lands of Badachache, lying in the barony of Rothienorman and shire of Aberdeen, to Stephen Clerk, his son-in-law, and Margaret his spouse, to be holden by them as freely and quietly as the said Andrew and his predecessors held the same of the said Sir Andrew de Leslie, and doing therefor to the king, chief lord of the said lands, the services used and wont, and giving to the said Andrew de Garvyack a penny money at the old manor-place of Kynbruyn yearly, for the ward, relief, marriages, escheats, and all other service for the said lands.

This charter is dated 14th April 1380, but the charter of confirmation by Sir Andrew de Leslie is without date.*

Sir Andrew de Leslie, VIII. Dominus Ejusdem, married, but no record has been found of the lady's name. By her he had a son, Norman, as is proved by deeds and transactions hereafter narrated.

It would appear that he had also another son, John, but the only records found concerning him are the following—viz. In some *Peerages*, under the title of Earls of Errol, it is stated that Margaret, second daughter of Sir Thomas Hay of Errol, Constable of Scotland, married John, son and heir of Sir Andrew de Leslie. This seems to be the marriage referred to in the discharge already mentioned, given, 12th July 1376, by Sir Andrew de Leslie to Sir Thomas de Haia for £200, on account of a contract of marriage between Sir Andrew's son and Sir Thomas's daughter. As no trace of this John, son and heir of Sir Andrew de Leslie, has been found in any of the family charters, it is probable that he died without issue at an early age.

Sir Andrew de Leslie, for some reason, perhaps from having arrived at an advanced age, about

---

* Manuscript Notes of Leslie Charters.

1389 resigned great part of his estates to his son Norman.

Norman married, but his wife's name and family are not recorded. By her he had a son, David, who, it seems, had gone abroad to the holy war in Palestine, and having been absent for several years without any tidings of him having reached home, he was supposed to be dead. Under this impression, Norman, in consequence of his father's resignation of the family estates to him, executed a deed of entail, settling certain estates on his own heirs-male, failing whom, on his consanguineus, *i.e.* cousin, Sir George Leslie of Rothes. In execution of this settlement, Norman Leslie resigned the barony of Ballinbreich in Fife, the barony of Lowr and Dunlopie in Forfarshire, and the baronies of Cushney and Rothienorman in Aberdeenshire, into the hands of King Robert II.; and at the last council held by Robert II. at Linlithgow, 1389, Norman received from the king a grant of the said lands in favour of himself and the heirs-male of his body, whom failing, of Sir George Leslie of Rothes. Norman Leslie afterwards got a charter from Robert III. dated at Scone, 18th August 1390, confirming to him the grant made by the deceased King Robert II. of the foresaid lands, to be holden by Norman, and the heirs-male of his body, whom failing, by Sir George Leslie, knight, and his heirs-male, whom failing, by the said Norman's lawful heirs whomsoever, in fee and heritage;

reserving nevertheless to the said Norman Leslie's father, Sir Andrew de Leslie, the free tenement and liferent of the whole lands during all the days of his life.

Sir Andrew.
See App. No. VIII.

Sir Andrew de Leslie, Dominus Ejusdem, and Norman de Leslie, his son and heir, entered into an agreement with Dominus Andreas de Leslie de Syde, the third Baron of Balquhain, whereby the said Sir Andrew and his son Norman, of one consent, give, grant, and confirm to the said Andrew de Leslie of Syde, their consanguineus or cousin, an annual rent of £13 : 6 : 8, to be paid out of the rents of the barony of Leslie within the regality of St. Andrews, or out of the lands and barony of Cushney in the shire of Aberdeen, at the option of the said Andrew de Leslie of Syde, to be received by him, by the bailies of the said Norman de Leslie, at the feasts of Whitsunday and Martinmas by equal portions, for his service and keeping, from the said Sir Andrew and Norman his son, and the longest liver of them, to be holden by the said Andrew de Leslie of Syde, for the whole term of his life, as freely and quietly as any other annual rent is held within the kingdom of Scotland. And the said Sir Andrew de Leslie and his son Norman did give and grant that, should the said Sir Andrew de Leslie of Syde want the payment of the said annual rent fourteen days after any term, he should be at liberty to poind the goods upon the said baronies aye and while he was completely paid what was due. And the said Sir Andrew and his son Norman oblige themselves to procure the confirmation of George de Leslie, Dominus de Rothes, upon the whole premises. The agreement is dated at Leslie, 24th November 1390.*

Sir Andrew de Leslie, Dominus Ejusdem, with the consent and assent of Norman de Leslie, his son and heir, granted to David de Abercrombie and Margaret de Leslie, his spouse, sister to the said Sir Andrew, a charter of the lands of Aquhorties, Acquhorsk, and Blairdaff, to be held by the said David and Margaret, and the longest liver of them, and by the heirs of their bodies; whom failing, to revert to the said Sir Andrew and his heirs whomsoever. The charter is dated 30th May 1391.

Norman Leslie died shortly after this, during the lifetime of his father Sir Andrew; and there being still no account of Norman's son David, Sir George Leslie of Rothes, the next substitute, on the supposition that David was dead, was served heir of entail to Norman, as is proved by a precept of Chancery, dated at Clerkingtown 7th January anno regni 2do Roberti II., A.D. 1391-2, proceeding upon the retour of George de Leslie, knight, consanguineus or cousin of the deceased Norman de Leslie, knight, as nearest and lawful

---

* See *Retour of Charters*, Signet Library, Edinburgh.

heir of tailzie to the said Norman in the baronies of Ballinbreich, Cushney, Rothienorman, etc., saving every one's right, and taking security for 200 merks as the relief of the said baronies, etc. But Sir George Leslie did not obtain possession of these lands during the lifetime of Sir Andrew de Leslie, Norman's father, as is proved by the following extract from the Chamberlain's accounts, rendered by Alexander Fraser, vicecomes de Aberdene, 1392 :—

"Et memorandum quod computans non oneratur ad presens de relevis quadraginta librorum debit., de baronia de Cushney, nec de viginta libris relevii debitis de baronia de Rothienorman per mortem Domini Normani de Lesley, domini earundem, filii scilicet Domini Andreae de Lesley, qui habet possessionem illarum terrarum in libero tenemento, pro tempore vitae suae : quae quidem relevia respectuanter quousque Dominus Georgius de Lesley nunc habens feodum illarum terrarum assecutus fuerit et adeptus liberum tenementum illarum terrarum cum feodo, et precipitur vicecomes quod tunc compellat."

King Robert III., 7th April 1392, granted a charter confirming a charter granted by the then deceased Norman de Leslie, knight, to Sir John Ramsay of Culathy, dated at Ballinbreich, 15th August 1390.

From these documents it is evident that Norman Leslie died after the 30th May 1391, when, with his consent, his father, Sir Andrew, granted the charter of Aquhorties, etc., to David de Abercrombie, and before the 7th January 1392, the date of the precept for serving Sir George Leslie as his heir of entail.

It appears that Sir Andrew de Leslie possessed other lands besides those which he assigned to his son Norman, as there is a charter in the charter-room of the Earls of Rothes, dated at Aberdeen, 24th October 1396, whereby Andrew de Leslie, knight, Dominus Ejusdem, dispones to his dear cousin, George de Leslie, knight, Dominus de Rothes, all right or claim which he had or could have, in any manner, in time coming, in the barony of Cairney in Perthshire, and the superiority thereof, without any gain-calling by him or his heirs for ever, promising, upon his good faith and under hypotheck of all his goods, to have the evidents of the said lands given to the said Sir George de Leslie and his heirs, whenever need shall be or it shall seem expedient.

Sir Andrew de Leslie, VIII. Dominus Ejusdem, died about 1398, and was succeeded by his grandson, David de Leslie.

IX. DAVID DE LESLIE,

DOMINUS EJUSDEM.

DAVID DE LESLIE, son of Norman de Leslie, and grandson of Sir Andrew de Leslie, VIII. Dominus

Ejusdem, succeeded his grandfather, as IX. Dominus Ejusdem, about 1398, his father Norman having died in 1391.

As has been related, David Leslie was abroad, engaged in the holy wars, when his father died, and being supposed dead, Sir George Leslie of Rothes was served as heir of entail to David's father Norman, 7th January 1391-2. It would appear that two or three years after the death of Sir Andrew de Leslie, VIII. Dominus Ejusdem, his grandson returned to Scotland, and succeeded as IX. Dominus Ejusdem, as is proved by an inquest held before the Sheriff of Fyfe and a jury, by which he was declared to be the next heir of entail to his grandfather.

When he obtained possession of his patrimonial estates, David de Leslie confirmed the deed of entail made by his father Norman in 1389, in favour of Sir George Leslie, Dominus de Fitekill. This charter of confirmation, preserved in the charter-room of the Earls of Rothes, is without date. It has the seal of David de Leslie appended to it, and has the labels for seven other seals, all which are broken away, having been the seals of the several witnesses, who are designed as follows: Robert, Duke of Albany, Earl of Fife and Monteith, Regent of Scotland; John, Earl of Brechin; William de Haya, Constable of Scotland; John Stewart of Lorn, knight; Alexander, Earl of Crawford; Gilbert, Bishop of Aberdeen; and

Henry, Bishop of St. Andrews. From the name of the Duke of Albany being among these witnesses, we learn that this charter of confirmation must have been granted between 1406 and 1420, during which time he was Regent of Scotland.

David de Leslie, Dominus Ejusdem, and Norman Leslie of Fitekill, son of Sir George Leslie of Rothes, were of the number of Scottish noblemen who were sent into England as hostages for the ransom of King James I. David de Leslie, Dominus de Leslie, had a safe conduct to Durham to meet the king, 13th December 1423.*

David de Leslie remained in England as a hostage till 20th June 1432, when Sir William Baillie of Hoprick was accepted as a substitute for him.†

David de Leslie, on his return to Scotland after his lengthened sojourn abroad, married Margaret, daughter of Sir Robert Davidson, chief magistrate of Aberdeen, who was killed at the battle of Harlaw, 24th July 1411. By her he had one child, Margaret, married to Alexander Leslie, son of Sir Andrew Leslie, third Baron of Balquhain.

In 1438, shortly before his death, David de Leslie again confirmed the deed of entail of his father Norman, entailing his principal estates on Norman de Leslie of Fitekill, son of Sir George

---

* *Rotuli Scotiæ*, vol. ii. p. 17.   † *Ibid.* p. 277.

Leslie of Rothes, now deceased, as heir-male, and he settled the barony of Leslie in the Garioch on his daughter Margaret, whose husband, Alexander Leslie, in her right took the title of Leslie of Leslie, or of that Ilk.*

David de Leslie, IX. Dominus Ejusdem, died in March 1439, at an advanced age, and was succeeded in his principal estates by Norman Leslie of Rothes and Fitekill, as is proved by an inquest ordered by Chancery to inquire what lands the deceased David de Leslie, knight, Dominus Ejusdem, consanguineus or cousin of Norman Leslie, the bearer thereof, died vest and seized in, and if the said Norman Leslie of Rothes and Fitekill was nearest and lawful heir-male to the said David by reason of the tailzie made in 1389. The brieve of inquest is dated at Edinburgh, the 2d May 1439, the third year of the reign of James II. The inquest was held at Cupar in Fife, 19th May 1439, before H. Warden, sheriff-depute. The jury unanimously agreed that the deceased David de Leslie, knight, died vest in the barony of Ballinbreich, and that Norman Leslie of Fitekill was the nearest lawful heir-male to the said David, his cousin, by reason of the tailzie aforesaid; and that the barony was worth 200 merks per annum; and found that the said barony was in the king's hands two months, because the heir of tailzie did

---

* *See* Note E.—Concerning child of David de Leslie by Margaret Davidson.

not set forth his right or claim for that time after the death of David de Leslie, in February or March 1439.

With David de Leslie, IX. Dominus Ejusdem, ended the direct line of the Dynasta de Leslie. After his death the extensive possessions of the family of Leslie were divided, and while the Leslies of that Ilk, the descendants of his daughter Margaret, became a minor branch of the family, the Leslies of Balquhain and the Leslies of Rothes became the principal branches. The splendour and magnificence which had adorned the stem now adorned these two great branches, Balquhain and Rothes. All the families of the name of Leslie now existing are cadets of these two branches, and the greater number of these families derive their origin from the family of Balquhain.*

---

* *See* Note F.—*Laurus Leslæana* account of David de Leslie.

NOTES TO CHAPTER I.

Note A.—Lordship of Abernethy.

The great lordship of Abernethy, of which the barony of Ballinbreich formed a part, was held by Orm, the son of Hugh, in the reign of Malcolm IV., about 1160, and also by grants from William the Lion, about 1190. Orm's son, Lawrence, assumed the name of Abernethy from his lands. He gave the Canons of the priory of St. Andrews ten shillings yearly, payable out of Ballinbreich, with the consent of Sir Patrick Abernethy, his son and heir, about 1230. Sir Patrick's son, Hugh de Abernethy, possessed great influence previous to and during the reign of Alexander III., about 1260. Sir Hugh de Abernethy died before 3d September 1296, as, on that date, we find that King Edward I. of England ordered the sheriff of Forfar to repone Maria, quæ fuit uxor Hugonis de Abernethy, in her lands. Sir Alexander de Abernethy succeeded his father, Sir Hugh. He swore fealty to Edward I., 10th July 1292, and again 25th June 1296, and adhered to the English interests. He was made warden of the country between the Forth and the mountains by Edward II. in 1310. He was one of the English plenipotentiaries appointed to treat with King Robert Bruce in 1312. He got a grant from Edward II. of the manor of Wyleighten, 3d May 1313. On the death of Sir Alexander de Abernethy the lordship of Abernethy was divided between his

CHAP. I.
Note A.

daughters and co-heiresses, Margaret, married to John Stuart, Earl of Angus, and Mary, married to Sir Andrew de Leslie, VI. Dominus Ejusdem.

Note B.

NOTE B.—"LAURUS LESLÆANA" ACCOUNT OF SIR ANDREW DE LESLIE'S MARRIAGE AND ISSUE.

THE *Laurus Leslæana* states that Sir Andrew de Leslie, VI. Dominus Ejusdem, married Elizabeth Douglas, daughter of Lord Douglas, whose successors became Marquises of Douglas, and with whom he got as her dowry the lands of Woodfield, now called Bomain, which in those days were reserved for hunting, as lying near the royal castles of Fettercairn and Kincairn, and that he had by her—

    I. JOHN, who succeeded him;
    II. GEORGE, to whom he gave the baronies of Syde and Balquhain, and who became the founder of that branch of the family of Leslie;
    III. MARGARET, married to Sir John Innes of Innes;
    IV. ANN, married to Sir Alexander Dunbar of Westfield.

It has been shown that these two ladies were the sisters, not the daughters, of Sir Andrew, being the daughters of Sir Norman de Leslie, V. Dominus Ejusdem. The *Laurus* is also decidedly wrong in giving the name of Sir Andrew's wife as Elizabeth Douglas instead of Mary Abernethy. That Sir Andrew de Leslie had a son John, who succeeded him, and who, according to the *Laurus*, married Lady Margaret Hay, daughter of Sir Thomas Hay of Errol, by whom he had a son, David, who succeeded him, and another son Norman, who became the founder of the Rothes family, is unquestionably a mistake, there being no mention of a John Leslie,

Dominus Ejusdem, in any of the public records or Peerages, and these details, as given by the *Laurus*, do not agree with the records of the time, and with known historical facts. A John Leslie is certainly mentioned in some Peerages as having married a daughter of Sir Thomas Hay of Errol in 1376, but he, as has been shown, was not the son, but the great-grandson of Sir Andrew de Leslie, VI. Dominus Ejusdem.

Note C.—Errors regarding Norman de Leslie.

It has been said that Norman de Leslie married Muriel de Pollock, daughter of Petrus de Pollock, and who was styled "Domina de Rothes;" and there is a charter in the chartulary of Arbroath, giving the succession of the Rothes family, which says that Sir Norman Leslie, brother of Walter Leslie, Earl of Ross, was the father of Sir George Leslie of Rothes. Others say that Norman de Leslie, brother of Walter, Earl of Ross, married the heiress of Taces in Fife, named Blair, and by her had a son, Sir George Leslie of Rothes. But these statements are evidently incorrect, as it has been shown that Norman de Leslie married Margaret Lamberton, who survived him. It has also been said that Norman de Leslie went with the Earl of Douglas to the Holy Land with the heart of King Robert Bruce in 1330.

Note D.—Letter addressed by Scottish Barons to Pope John XXII.

Tytler, in his *History of Scotland*, vol. i. p. 140, ed. 1864, gives the following account of the letter addressed by the Scottish Barons to Pope John XXII.—

CHAP. I.
Note D.

"Some time after the final settlement of the truce (between England and Scotland), the Archbishop of York, with the Bishops of London and Carlisle, were commanded—and the order is stated to have proceeded on information communicated by Edward—to excommunicate Robert and his accomplices on every Sabbath and festival-day throughout the year. Convinced by this conduct that their enemies had been busy in misrepresenting, at the Roman court, their causes of quarrel with England, the Scottish nobility assembled in parliament at Aberbrothock, and with consent of the king, the barons, freeholders, and whole community of Scotland, directed a letter or manifesto to the Pope in a strain different from that servility of address to which the spiritual sovereign had been accustomed. After an exordium, in which they shortly allude to the then commonly-believed traditions regarding the emigration of the Scots from Scythia—their residence in Spain—and subsequent conquest of the Pictish kingdom: to their long line of a hundred and thirteen kings (many of whom are undoubtedly fabulous), to their conversion to Christianity by St. Andrew, and the privileges which they had enjoyed at the hands of their spiritual father, as the flock of the brother of St. Peter; they describe, in the following energetic terms, the unjust aggression of Edward the First:—

"Under such free protection did we live, until Edward, king of England and father of the present monarch, covering his hostile designs under the specious disguise of friendship and alliance, made an invasion of our country at a moment when it was without a king, and attacked an honest and unsuspicious people—then but little experienced in war. The insults which this prince has heaped upon us, the slaughters and devastations which he has committed, his imprisonments of prelates, his burning of monasteries, his spoliations and murder of priests, and other enormities of which he has been guilty, can be rightly described or even conceived by none but an eyewitness. From these innumerable evils we have been freed, under the help of that God who woundeth and who maketh whole, by our most valiant prince and king Lord Robert, who, like a second Maccabæus or Joshua, hath cheerfully endured all labour and weariness, and exposed himself to every species of danger and privation, that he might rescue from the hands of the enemy his ancient people and rightful inheritance, whom also Divine Providence and the right of succession, according to those laws and customs which we will maintain to the death, as well as the common consent of all, have made our prince and king. To him we are bound, both by his own merit and by the law of the land, and to him, as the saviour of our people and the guardian of our liberty, are we unanimously determined to adhere; but if he should desist from what he has begun, and should show an inclination to subject us or our kingdom to the king of England or to his people, then we declare that we will use our utmost effort to expel him from the throne as our enemy and the subverter of his own and of our right, and we will choose another king to rule over us, who will be able to defend us; for as long as a hundred Scotsmen are left alive we will never be subject to the dominion of England. It is not for glory, riches, or honour, that we fight, but for that liberty which no good man will consent to lose but with his life. Wherefore, most reverend Father, we humbly pray,.and from our hearts, beseech your Holiness to consider that you are the vicegerent of Him with whom there is no respect of persons, Jews or Greeks, Scots or English; and turning your paternal regard upon the tribulations brought upon us and the Church of God by the English, to admonish the king of England that he should be content with what he possesses, seeing that England of old was enough for seven or more kings, and not to disturb our peace in this small country, lying on the utmost boundaries of the habitable earth, and whose inhabitants desire nothing but what is their own."

The barons proceed to say that they are willing to do everything for peace which may not compromise the freedom of their constitution and government, and they exhort the Pope to procure the peace of Christendom, in order to the removal of all impediments in the way of a crusade against the infidels, declaring the readiness with which they and their king would undertake that sacred warfare if the king of England would cease to disturb them. Their conclusion is exceedingly spirited:—

"If," say they, "your Holiness do not sincerely believe these things, giving too implicit faith to the tales of the English, and on this ground shall not cease to favour them in their designs for our destruction, be well assured that the Almighty will impute to you that loss of life, that destruction of human souls, and all those various calamities, which our inextinguishable hatred against the English, and their warfare against us, must necessarily produce. Confident that we now are, and shall ever, as in duty bound, remain, obedient sons to you, as God's vicegerent, we commit the defence of our cause to that God, as the great King and Judge, placing our confidence in Him; and in the firm hope

THE FAMILY OF LESLIE. 43

that He will endow us with strength, and confound our enemies; and may the Almighty long preserve your Holiness in health."

This memorable letter is dated at Aberbrothock, on the 6th of April 1320, and it is signed by eight earls and thirty-one barons, amongst whom we find the great officers, the high steward, the seneschal, the constable, and the marshall, with the barons, freeholders, and whole community of Scotland.

NOTE E.—CONCERNING CHILD OF DAVID DE LESLIE BY HIS WIFE MARGARET DAVIDSON.

ACCORDING to some accounts, David de Leslie had a son, Alexander, by his wife Margaret Davidson. But this does not appear probable, since, as has been related, David de Leslie twice confirmed the deed of entail executed by his father Norman, in virtue of which Norman Leslie of Fitekill succeeded to the barony of Ballinbreich, as nearest heir-male, which he would not have been if David de Leslie had had a son.

NOTE F.—"LAURUS LESLÆANA" ACCOUNT OF DAVID DE LESLIE.

THE *Laurus Leslæana* says that David de Leslie succeeded his father John as Dominus Ejusdem, and that he married Elizabeth Leith of Edingarioch, and got with her Earlyfield, Premnay, and other lands; and that, seeing he had no issue, and no reason to expect any, he made over his estates to his brother Norman, on condition that should he survive his wife and marry again and have children, the estates should revert to him, and

CHAP. I.
Note F.

devolve on such children; and that after this, although in declining years, he went to Palestine, and served as a volunteer in the holy wars against the Saracens, and remained abroad seven years; and that, on his return home, finding that his wife was dead, he married, in the eightieth year of his age, as his second wife, Margaret Davidson, daughter of Sir Robert Davidson, Provost of Aberdeen, by whom he had a son, Alexander; and that he then wished to recover his estates, but his brother Norman, having so long enjoyed them, was unwilling to part with the whole; and that it was at last finally arranged that Alexander, David's son, should inherit the barony of Leslie in the Garioch, and that Norman should retain Fechill, Tasses, and other lands in Fife, with the rest of the southern possessions. There is no evidence to support these statements of the *Laurus Leslœana*, and the history of David de Leslie, IX. Dominus Ejusdem, given above, seems to be the true one, and is corroborated by public records and documents.

CHAPTER II.

ALEXANDER LESLIE,

FIRST BARON OF LESLIE, OR OF THAT ILK.

Alexander, First Baron of Leslie.

As has been related, David, IX. Dominus Ejusdem, had a daughter Margaret, to whom, at his death in March 1439, he left the barony of Leslie in the Garioch, and other lands in Aberdeenshire; while Norman Leslie of Rothes and Fythkill, son of Sir George Leslie of Rothes, succeeded to the barony of Ballinbreich, Tacis, and others, as the nearest heir-male under the deed of tailzie executed in 1389 by Norman Leslie, son of Andrew de Leslie, VIII. Dominus Ejusdem, and father of David, IX. Dominus Ejusdem.

Margaret Leslie married Alexander Leslie, son of Sir Andrew Leslie, third Baron of Balquhain, who in all public documents is styled Baron of Leslie, or of that Ilk. Alexander Leslie de Eodem, or of that Ilk, is a witness to a charter of half of the lands of Westhall, granted by Alexander Ramsay of Westhall to his brother Edward Ramsay, dated at the chapel of the Virgin Mary in the

Garioch, 26th May 1453.* Alexander de Leslie, Dominus Ejusdem, granted a charter of the lands of Braco, Cults, Milltown of Knockinlews, and Drummies, with their pertinents, lying in the barony of Leslie and regality of the Garioch, to William Leslie, fourth Baron of Balquhain, 27th March 1460.

By his first wife, Margaret Leslie, Alexander Leslie had issue—

I. JOHN, who, it was said, was poisoned by his stepmother;
II. JOHANNA, married to Strachan, a brother of the Baron of Thornton.

Alexander Leslie married, secondly, Janet Mowat, a daughter of the Baron of Baldquhollie, by whom he had issue—

I. WILLIAM, born in 1430, who is documented by an obligation dated at Leslie Castle in the Garioch, 10th July 1458, whereby Alexander Leslie of that Ilk obliged himself to George, first Earl of Rothes, Lord Leslie upon Leven, that if the marriage appointed betwixt William Leslie, son and heir-apparent of the said Alexander, or any other of the said Alexander's sons and apparent heirs, and Lady Margaret Leslie, the daughter of the said Earl of Rothes by Margaret Lundin, his spouse, or any other of the said Earl's daughters, did not take place through the default of the said Alexander Leslie, or of his sons, then to pay to the said Earl the sum of 500 merks, besides costs, skaith, and expenses in recovering the same. It would appear that William Leslie died during the lifetime of his father.
II. GEORGE, who succeeded as second Baron of that Ilk.

Alexander Leslie, first Baron of that Ilk, died

---

* See *Registrum Episcopatus Aberdonensis*, vol. i. p. 240.

about 1470, and was succeeded by his eldest surviving son, George Leslie, second Baron of that Ilk.

GEORGE LESLIE,

SECOND BARON OF THAT ILK.

GEORGE LESLIE, born in 1432, succeeded his father Alexander Leslie, as second Baron of that Ilk, about 1470.

George Leslie of that Ilk is witness to a decree of Sir William* Leslie, fourth Baron of Balquhain, as bailie to our Sovereign Lady the Queen, in the regality of the Garioch, giving possession of half of the lands of Drumdurnoch to John Winton, dated at Wardis, 23d May 1453.* He was one of the jury in the service of Thomas, Lord Erskine, in the half of the earldom of Mar, 5th November 1457.† He was witness to a bond of manrent between William, brother-german to George, Earl of Rothes, and William, Earl of Errol, dated 3d June 1490.‡ He sold the lands of Edingarioch and others to William Leith, second son of Henry Leith of Barnes, and granted a charter of the same to him, 31st January 1499.§ Between 1490 and 1500 he resigned the lands of Braco, Middletown, Knockinlews, Drummies,

---

* See *Collections on Shires of Aberdeen and Banff*, p. 141.
† *Miscellanies of Spalding Club*, vol. v. p. 271.
‡ *Ibid.* vol. ii. p. 260.   § *See* Douglas' *Baronage*, p. 225.

CHAP. II.
George, Second Baron of Leslie.
See App. No. XI.

Glaschawe, Mill of Glaschawe, and the wood of Drumcontane, in the regality of the Garioch, into the hands of the king, in favour of Patrick Gordon of Methlic. King James IV., by a charter dated at Stirling 31st August 1505, erected these lands into a free barony in favour of Patrick Gordon. George Leslie of that Ilk was one of the jurors in an inquisition held at Aberdeen, 7th January 1505, regarding the title of Elizabeth Ouchtirarne to the lands of Ouchtirarne in the earldom of Mar;* and on the same day he was on the assize for appraising the lands of Stoneywood. He was on another assize, held at Aberdeen 12th January 1506, and on another, held at Aberdeen 5th June 1507, anent the spoliation of oxen from the lands of Fyvie. He also attended the head court, held at Aberdeen 3d October 1508.

George Leslie married, first, Lady Christian Leslie, daughter of George, first Earl of Rothes, as is shown by an obligation, dated 20th May 1478, whereby George Leslie of that Ilk, acknowledging the great kindness which the Earl of Rothes had shown to him, in upholding him at great expense, from his childhood till he was twenty-one years of age, and had paid great sums of money for his marriage with Lady Christian Leslie, daughter of the said Earl of Rothes, therefore he bound himself not to sell or wadsett any of his lands, or any that he was heir to, and

---

* *Antiquities of Shires of Aberdeen and Banff*, vol. ii. p. 11.

THE FAMILY OF LESLIE.

that he would not alienate any part of his lands from the heir to be procreate betwixt him and the said Lady Christina Leslie. By this marriage George Leslie had issue—

>   I. ALEXANDER, who succeeded as third Baron of that Ilk;
>   II. GEORGE, who died without issue;
>   III. BEATRIX, who died without issue.

George Leslie married, secondly, in 1497, Violet Middleton. George Leslie of that Ilk, and Violet Middleton his spouse, got a charter of half of the lands of Edingarioch and half of the lands of Chapeltown, from King James IV., 24th November 1497. By Violet Middleton he had issue—

>   I. HENRY, who married and had a son, William Leslie, who had several sons and daughters;
>   II. JOHN;
>   III. JANET, married to James Davidson, with whom she went to Copenhagen, and died there.

George Leslie married, thirdly, Margaret Fraser, daughter of the Baron of Muchals. King James IV. confirmed a charter to George Leslie of that Ilk, and Margaret Fraser his spouse, of eight mercates of the lands of Chapeltoune in the lordship of the Garioch, 26th October 1505. By Margaret Fraser George Leslie had issue—

>   I. THOMAS, who died a student at Edinburgh;
>   II. WILLIAM, styled Goodman of Chapeltown. He married Lucretia Innis, daughter of Innis of that Ilk, by whom he had issue—
>   >   I. BARTHOLOMEW;
>   >   II. PATRICK.

George Leslie, second Baron of that Ilk, died before 1513, and was succeeded by his eldest son, Alexander Leslie, third baron of that Ilk.

ALEXANDER LESLIE,

THIRD BARON OF THAT ILK.

ALEXANDER LESLIE, eldest son of George Leslie, second Baron of that Ilk, by Lady Christina Leslie, his spouse, succeeded as third Baron of that Ilk, on the death of his father before 1513.

Alexander Leslie of that Ilk, as superior of the lands of Aquhorties, Aquhorsk, and Blairdaff, granted a precept of sasine in favour of William Mortimer of Craigievar, in the half of the said lands, 28th September 1513.*

Alexander Leslie of that Ilk was one of the Barons who joined William Leslie, seventh Baron of Balquhain, in attacking the town of Aberdeen, and slaying several of the citizens, 1st October 1525, as appears from the following extracts from the *Council Register of the Burgh of Aberdeen*, "2d October 1525.—The said day, the prowest, ballies, and counsell, with consent and assent of all the haill communite, thei beand circualie inquirit be the officiaris, na maner of person opponand nor sayand in the contrar, maid, creat,

---

* Balquhain Charters, No. 255.

THE FAMILY OF LESLIE.

and ordanit rycht honourable men, that is to say, Thomas Menzes of Pitfoddellis, thar prowest for the tyme, Gilbert Menzes of Fyndoun, Sir Johnne Rutherford, Andro Cullan, and William Rolland, thair veire lauchfull and undoutit commissaris, to set and prolong all and syndrie their fischings and takis, baitht to burgh and to land now waikind and beand in thair handis, to burges and induellars the said burgh now actuallie, and to nane uthers, and to nae maner of person quhilks wes art or part of the cruell murther, slauchter, mutilatioun, and hunting of their nychtbours, prowest, baillies, and officiaris, maid on thame under silence of nycht be Alex^r. Setoun of Meldrum, Johnne Leslie of Wardors, Willzeame Leslie of Bognhane, Alex^r. Leslie of that Ilk, thair sonns and ayris, complecis and pairt takaris, to the nomer of iiii^{xx} speirs, or thereby, be solstation of Johnne Collison eldar, and his complesces, with power to the saids commissaris to set the said tacks and fisching for five years immediate followand the vigill of Sanct Androw nixt to cum, and thair commissoun to be maid under thair commund seill to the said commissaris, in the largest forme, to this effect."*

Alexander Leslie married Janet Leslie, daughter of George Leslie, first Baron of New Leslie. Janet Leslie, spouse of Alexander Leslie of that Ilk, got

---

* Extracts from the *Burgh Records of Aberdeen*.

a charter from King James V. 27th November 1526. By her Alexander Leslie had issue—

I. CHRISTINA, who succeeded him in the barony of Leslie;
II. MARGARET. On the 21st January 1544, Alexander Leslie, fourth Baron of that Ilk, in his own name, and in the name of John Leslie, his eldest son and heir, went to the personal presence of Miss Margaret Leslie, daughter of the deceased Alexander Leslie of that Ilk, and offered to her John Leslie his brother-german, or Mr. Thomas Mortimer, as a fit husband for her, whomsoever of the two she might choose, and promised to obtain a dispensation for the marriage if they were within the forbidden degrees of kindred; and if she refused to marry either of these two, and married any one else, the said Alexander Leslie would enter a legal protest.

Besides these, Alexander Leslie had seven sons and six daughters, who all died young.

Alexander Leslie, third Baron of that Ilk, was succeeded by his eldest daughter Christina, married to Alexander Leslie of Pitnamoon, who, in right of his wife, became fourth Baron of Leslie, about 1520.

ALEXANDER LESLIE,

FOURTH BARON OF THAT ILK.

CHRISTINA LESLIE, eldest daughter of Alexander Leslie, third Baron of that Ilk, succeeded her father in the barony of Leslie. She married Alexander Leslie, second son of George Leslie of Pitnamoon, and he, in right of his wife, became fourth Baron of Leslie. He also succeeded his nephew George in

THE FAMILY OF LESLIE.

the lands of Pitnamoon. The issue of this marriage was—

I. JOHN, who succeeded as fifth Baron of Leslie;
II. WALTER.

Alexander Leslie and Christina Leslie, his spouse, fiars of the barony of Leslie, with the consent of Janet Leslie, liferenter of the barony, sold to John Awaill, Alexander Wrycht, Duncan Robertson, and David Barnys, and the other chaplains of the choir of the Collegiate Church of Aberdeen, and their successors, an annual rent of forty shillings out of the manor of Leslie, and gave in warrandice thereof the lands of the barony of Pitnamoon, lying in the barony of Balmain and shire of Kincardine, 9th August 1527. As has been related, Alexander Leslie of that Ilk, in his own name, and in the name of his son and heir John, offered to his sister-in-law Margaret Leslie, daughter of the deceased Alexander Leslie of that Ilk, either his own brother-german John Leslie, or Master Thomas Mortimer, as a suitable husband for her, and if she refused to marry either of these two, he entered a legal protest against her marriage with any one else, 21st January 1544.

Alexander Leslie of that Ilk was one of the assize of Lords and Barons convened at Aberdeen, 16th June 1548, by John Leslie, eighth Baron of Balquhain, sheriff-depute of Aberdeen, in virtue of a warrant from Queen Mary, to make a rate and

CHAP. II.
Alexander, Fourth Baron of Leslie.

See App. No. XIV.

1527.

See App. No. XV.

1544.

1548.

to tax all the lands within the shire of Aberdeen.*
Alexander Leslie of that Ilk, superior of the sunny half of the lands of Aquhorties, the sunny half of Overtown, the sunny half of Netherbeggery, the sunny half of Woodhill, the sunny half of Blairdaff, and half of the mill thereof, granted a charter of the said lands to John Leslie, eighth Baron of Balquhain, 26th February 1554.†

Alexander Leslie, fourth Baron of that Ilk, was succeeded by his eldest son, John Leslie, fifth Baron of that Ilk.

JOHN LESLIE,

FIFTH BARON OF THAT ILK.

JOHN LESLIE, eldest son of Alexander Leslie of Pitnamoon, fifth Baron of Leslie, by his wife Christina Leslie, succeeded as fifth Baron of Leslie on the death of his father.

John, abbot of Lindores, with the consent of the monks, granted a lease for nineteen years of the teind-sheaves of the Mains of Leslie, Auld Leslie, and Curtastoun, to John Leslie of that Ilk, and Elizabeth Dempster his spouse, for the sum of £30 Scots, and a yearly rent of forty-two merks—to wit, nine merks for the teind-sheaves of the Mains of Leslie, thirteen merks for the teind-sheaves of Auld Leslie, and twenty merks for the

---

* *Collections on Shires of Aberdeen and Banff*, p. 115.
† Balquhain Charters, No. 257.

teind-sheaves of Curtaston, payable yearly at the feast of St. Lawrence the martyr, or at the feast of St. Bartholomew, 10th October 1546. John Leslie of that Ilk granted a precept of clare constat in favour of Gilbert Leith of Barnes, 10th May 1548.* He also granted a precept to infeft William Leslie younger, afterwards ninth Baron of Balquhain, in the lands of Aquhorties, Woodhill, Blairdaff, and others, 4th October 1560.† Sir Thomas Raith, vicar of the parish church of Leslie, with the consent of John, abbot of Lindores, and of the monks of the same, granted a feu-charter of the kirklands and glebe of the vicarage of Leslie to John Leslie of that Ilk, for a certain sum of money, and a yearly duty of four merks, and also two shillings in augmentation of the rental, and ordered his bailies, Robert Leslie in Auchmair and Nicholas Murray, to give sasine in the said lands to the said John Leslie; but reserving to himself and his successors the manse of the said vicarage, and the sowing of two bolls of barley in the east part of the croft of Gostach, 1st May 1561. John Leslie of that Ilk, with other barons, signed a bond to support Queen Mary's authority under the Earl of Huntly, her Lieutenant of the North, in 1568.‡ John Leslie,

---

* Charter in possession of Mr. Grant Leslie, Sheriff-clerk depute, Aberdeen.
† Balquhain Charters, No. 258.
‡ Gordon Papers, *Miscellany of Spalding Club*, vol. iv. p. 157.

CHAP. II.
John, Fifth Baron of Leslie.
See App. No. XVIII.

1579.

1586.

1589.

1543.

vicar of Pramoth, granted to John Leslie of that Ilk, a lease for twice nineteen years of the teinds of the Mains of Leslie, and of the lands of Edingarioch, in so far as lies within the parish of Premnay—that is to say, teind-hay, teind-nolt, teind-cheis, teind-lint, and all other emoluments pertaining to the vicarage—for the annual rent of forty shillings Scots, payable at the feast of Pasch, 27th January 1579. John Leslie of that Ilk conveyed the kirklands and glebe of the vicarage of Leslie to his grandson, John Leslie, son of Patrick Leslie, by his wife Isabella, daughter of John Leslie of that Ilk, in 1584. John Leslie of that Ilk granted a precept of infeftment to George Leith of Barnes, dated at Leslie Castle, 7th November 1586. John Leslie of that Ilk got a charter of the barony of Leslie from King James VI., 30th May 1589.*

John Leslie, fifth Baron of that Ilk, married Elizabeth Dempster, daughter of Dempster of Muiresk. John Leslie of that Ilk, and Elizabeth Dempster his spouse, got a charter of the barony of Leslie from Queen Mary, 28th July 1543.† By Elizabeth Dempster John Leslie had issue—

I. PATRICK, who succeeded as sixth Baron of Leslie;
II. ISABELLA, who was married to Patrick Leslie, and had a son, John.

He had also several other sons and daughters,

---

* *Registrum Magni Sigilli*, lib. xlv. No. 149.
† *Ibid.* lib. xxix. No. 154.

who all died without issue. He was succeeded by his son Patrick Leslie, sixth Baron of that Ilk.

PATRICK LESLIE,

SIXTH BARON OF THAT ILK.

PATRICK LESLIE, son of John Leslie, fifth Baron of that Ilk, by Elizabeth Dempster his wife, succeeded as sixth Baron of that Ilk on the death of his father.

Patrick Leslie married, first, Margaret Lumsden, daughter of Robert Lumsden, bailie of Aberdeen; she died 20th August 1575, as appears from the following extract from the *Chronicle of Aberdeen:*

"Margrett Lumisden, lady of Lesly, and doithar to Maister Robert Lumsden, Bailye of Aberdeen, departtit in the Garioche the xx. day of Aguist, the yeir of God 1575 yeirs."*

Patrick Leslie married, secondly, Sarah Keith, as is proved by a deed whereby their son, George Leslie, with the consent of his mother Sarah Keith, disponed the lands and barony of Leslie to John Forbes in 1618. By her he had issue—

I. JOHN, who succeeded as seventh Baron of Leslie;
II. GEORGE, who succeeded his brother John as eighth Baron of Leslie;
III. ALEXANDER, who died before 19th August 1618, when his brother George was served heir to him; †

---

* *Miscellanies, Spalding Club*, vol. ii. p. 42.
† *Antiquities of Aberdeen and Banff*, vol. iii. p. 393.

IV. MARGARET, who was served heir-portioner to her father Patrick Leslie of that Ilk, 14th February 1604;*

V. JANET, who with her sister Margaret, was served heir-portioner to her father, Patrick Leslie of that Ilk, as above.†

Patrick Leslie, sixth Baron of that Ilk, appears to have died about 1601, and was succeeded by his eldest son, John Leslie, seventh Baron of that Ilk.

JOHN LESLIE,

SEVENTH BARON OF THAT ILK.

JOHN LESLIE, eldest son of Patrick Leslie, sixth Baron of that Ilk, by Sarah Keith, his wife, succeeded as seventh Baron of Leslic on the death of his father, about 1601.

John Leslie of that Ilk, as superior of the lands of Barnes, granted an instrument of sasine in favour of Gilbert Leith in the lands of Barnes, 8th May 1601.‡

John Leslie, seventh Baron of that Ilk, died without issue before 5th April 1608, when his brother, George Leslie, eighth Baron of that Ilk, was served heir to him.

---

* "Inquisitiones Generales," No. 156. † *Ibid.* No. 157.
‡ Charter in possession of Mr. Grant Leslie, Sheriff-clerk depute, Aberdeen.

GEORGE LESLIE,

EIGHTH BARON OF THAT ILK.

GEORGE LESLIE, second son of Patrick Leslie, sixth Baron of that Ilk, by Sarah Keith, his wife, succeeded his elder brother John as eighth Baron of that Ilk, and was served heir to him, 5th April 1608, in the barony of Leslie, in the superiority of the shady half of the town and lands of Aquhorsk, in the barony of Leslie; in the lands of Auld Leslie, Chappeltown, Towleyis, with the mills; the half of the lands of Edingarioch, and the superiority of the other half; the superiority of the half of the lands of Aquhorties, and mill; Auchquhorsk, Blairdaff, the superiority of the lands of Erlisfeild, Newlandis, Bairnis, Cultis, New Leslie, and in the patronage of the benefices in the barony of Leslie.*

On the 19th August 1618 he was also served heir to Alexander Leslie of that Ilk, his brother,† to John Leslie of that Ilk, his grandfather, in the kirklands and glebe of the vicarage of Leslie,‡ and to Alexander Leslie of that Ilk, his great-grandfather.

---

* "Inquisitiones Speciales Vicecomitatus Aberdonensis," No. 115.—*Antiquities of Shires of Aberdeen and Banff*, vol. iii. p. 387.
† "Inquisitiones Generales," No. 770.
‡ "Inquisitiones Speciales, Abdn.," No. 158.

CHAP. II.

George, Eighth Baron of Leslie.

In 1608 George Leslie of that Ilk wadsett certain lands in the barony of Leslie to James Leslie of Chapeltown, and in 1616 he brought an action in the Court of Session for the redemption of the said lands. The Court of Session, 8th February 1616, sustained the reversion contained in the contract of wadsett dated 1608, but not registered until 1616.* George Leslie of that Ilk, as superior of half of the lands of Aquhorties, Overtown, and Nethertown of Aquhorties, Blairdaff, and Woodhill, granted a charter of the said lands to John Leslie, fiar, afterwards eleventh Baron of Balquhain, 21st March 1610, proceeding on the resignation of John Leslie, tenth Baron of Balquhain, 21st January 1610.

1616.

1610.

George Leslie of that Ilk and John Leslie of Pitcaple involved themselves in certain liabilities for James Leslie of Otterston. They became cautioners and securities for him in a bond of 1000 marks to Thomas Machray of Leithhills, and Agnes Grey his spouse, under a penalty of 300 merks failing payment, 15th June 1614. This bond was assigned by Thomas Machray to Patrick Leslie, burgess of Aberdeen, 29th May 1615, and he assigned it to Thomas Ramsay of Borghouse, 15th December 1615, who again assigned it to John Forbes of Enzean, second son of William Forbes of Monymusk, 1st June 1617. It seems

1614.

1615.

1617.

---

* *Decrees and Decisions,* vols. xxxi. xxxii. p. 13,443.

THE FAMILY OF LESLIE.

that George Leslie of that Ilk had become security for a great many bonds granted by James Leslie of Otterston, to various people, and these bonds were concentrated by various acquisitions in the person of Thomas Ramsay of Borghouse, who executed a general assignation of the whole bonds on the barony of Leslie in favour of John Forbes of Enzean. Under this assignation John Forbes obtained a decreet apprizing the barony of Leslie, 2d May 1618. In consequence of this decreet of apprizing, George Leslie, with the consent of Sarah Keith his mother, of Alexander Leslie his brother, and of John Leslie of Auld Leslie, executed a disposition of the barony of Leslie in favour of John Forbes of Enzean, 18th July 1618, and resigned the same into the King's hands in favour of John Forbes, who got a charter of the lands of Auchinleck and of the barony of Leslie from King James VI., 22d January 1619.

John Forbes of Enzean thus became baron of Leslie. It does not appear from the documents which have been examined what sum of money he paid for the barony. The contract of sale, contained in the disposition granted by George Leslie of that Ilk, with the consent of his mother and brother, 18th July 1618, is only referred to incidentally in a letter of inhibition and arrestment, proceeding on the contract, at the instance of John Forbes against George Leslie in 1620, to implement the contract. It would seem that

CHAP. II.

George, Eighth Baron of Leslie.

1618.

1619.

1620.

George Leslie, in reconsidering the transaction, had thought that he had made a bad bargain, and had refused to implement it; and that John Forbes had raised an action against him, and had gained his suit.

While George Leslie of that Ilk thus lost the estates of his ancestors, he still retained the superiority of the various lands which had belonged to him. As superior of the lands of Barnes, he granted a precept of sasine in the lands of Barnes in favour of George Leith, 26th January 1622. He pursued John Leslie of Pitcaple, who held certain lands of him by service of ward and relief, for the payment of the duties of all the years of the ward, and of all the years during the non-entry of the heir-apparent after the expiry of the ward. The Court of Session found that the superior of the said lands, George Leslie of that Ilk, could not bring an action for the duties of any year, during non-entry, before he obtained a decreet finding the lands in non-entry, 23d March 1622.* George Leslie, as superior, again pursued John Leslie of Pitcaple, his vassal, for payment of the duties of his lands during the time of the ward and non-entry of his lands following the ward. It was urged by Pitcaple that during the non-entry after ward the superior had no right to the duties of the lands, but only to the old extent, or retour duty, because the su-

---
* *Decisions and Decrees*, vols. xxi. xxii. p. 9289.

perior, before declaration, can claim no more. The Court of Session, 22d July 1626, found the defence relevant, seeing that the superior was not in succession.* George Leslie of that Ilk, as superior of the half of the lands of Aquhorties, obtained a decreet of recognition of the said lands against John Leslie, eleventh Baron of Balquhain, and John Leslie of Pitcaple, 7th July 1627, and he assigned the decreet to James Leslie, second son of the said John Leslie of Pitcaple, 10th July 1627; and, on the same day, he granted a charter of the said lands to the said James Leslie.† He granted a precept of clare constat in favour of John Leslie of Pitcaple, as heir to his father Duncan Leslie of Pitcaple in the shady half of the town and lands of Aquhorsk, lying in the barony of Leslie, 10th July 1627.‡ George Leslie of that Ilk was served heir of Malcolm Leslie, the great-great-great-great-grandfather of the great-great-great-great-grandfather of his father (tritavi tritavi patris), of Norman Leslie, the great-great-great-great-grandfather of his great-great-great-great-grandfather, and of Norman Leslie, the great-great-great-great-grandfather of his great-great-grandfather, 27th January 1632.§

---

* *Decisions and Decrees*, vols. xxi. xxii. p. 9304.
† Balquhain Charters, Nos. 307-309.
‡ *Antiquities of Aberdeen and Banff*, vol. iii. p. 387.
§ "Inquisitiones Generales," Nos. 1863, 1864, 1865.—*Antiquities of Shires of Aberdeen and Banff*, vol. iii. p. 393.

George Leslie of that Ilk, as superior of the sunny half of the lands of Aquhorties, granted a charter of the same in favour of William Robertson elder, and William Robertson younger. George Leslie of that Ilk got a charter of the lands of New Leslie, Brigs, Cults, and others, from King James VI., 2d March 1624.*

George Leslie of that Ilk married Catherine Henderson, by whom he had issue a son—

> I. JOHN, who was served heir to his mother, Mrs. Catherine Henderson, spouse of George Leslie of that Ilk, 26th August 1646.†

No farther accounts have been obtained of George Leslie, eighth and last baron of that Ilk, or of his son John.

It is stated in the *Laurus Leslæana*, and by others, that George Leslie, eighth Baron of Leslie, married the Honourable Jane Leslie, daughter of Lord Lindores; and that, after his death, his widow married John Forbes, who purchased the heavy debts on the estate and thus got possession of it. But this account is clearly refuted by the transactions and deeds above recorded.

---

* *Registrum Magni Sigilli*, lib. xlix. No. 324.
† "Inquisitiones Generales," No. 3183.

CHAPTER III.

WALTER LESLIE,

EARL OF ROSS.

Walter, Earl of Ross.

WALTER LESLIE, who became Earl of Ross in right of his wife Eufamia, Countess of Ross, daughter and heiress of William, sixth Earl of Ross, was the fourth son of Sir Andrew de Leslie, VI. Dominus Ejusdem, by his wife Mary Abernethy, daughter and co-heiress of Sir Alexander Abernethy of Abernethy.

See App. No. XIX.

John Leslie, Bishop of Ross, in his *Rebus Gestis Scotorum*, p. 201, states that Walter Leslie served in the Imperial army under the Emperors Louis IV. and Charles IV. (1346-1378), with great distinction, against the Saracens, and was so esteemed for his bravery against the enemy, and for his humanity towards the vanquished, that he was styled the "Generous Knight." The *Laurus Leslæana* styles him "Walter the Wight Leslie." Walter Leslie seems to have gone to the wars in Germany in 1356, as he and his brother Norman had a safe-conduct to pass through England on

1346-78.

1356.

their way to Prussia, 20th August 1356.*
Afterwards Walter Leslie returned to Scotland, but he did not remain long there. He went abroad again, and entered the service of the King of France. He got a safe-conduct into England for himself and sixty persons in his suite, going to foreign parts, 24th October 1358. He served with great distinction in the wars against King Edward III. of England. In reward of his services, Charles V. King of France, by a letter patent dated 1st October 1372, granted to Walter Leslie, Earl of Ross in the kingdom of Scotland, an annuity of 200 francs of gold, to be paid out of the Royal Treasury, for his good and faithful services against our ancient enemies of England, especially at the battle of Pontvalain. For this pension Walter de Leslie did homage to the King of France against all and every one, reserving the fidelity due by him to the King of Scotland and the Duke of Austria. The patent is in the possession of M. Letellier of Paris, as appears by a letter written by M. Teulet, sub-director of the Archives du Royaume, Palais de Soubise, to Colonel Charles Leslie, K. H. of Balquhain, 7th October 1845.

After such distinguished services abroad, Walter Leslie returned to Scotland before 1363. The fame of his exploits gained him the favour of

---

* *Rotuli Scotiæ*, vol. i. p. 797.

THE FAMILY OF LESLIE. 67

King David II., who, 14th October 1363, granted him a pension for life of forty pounds sterling, to be paid annually out of the great Customs of Dundee by the Chamberlain of Scotland.* Also, through the influence and friendship of King David II., Walter Leslie obtained in marriage Eufamia, eldest daughter and heiress of William, sixth Earl of Ross. The Lady Eufamia was a near relation of the king, and married Walter Leslie about 1365, as is shown by a charter granted by David II. to Walter de Leslie, knight, and Eufamia de Ross his spouse, of the new forest in the shire of Dumfries, to be held of the king in free barony, dated at Perth, 13th September 1365.† It appears that a papal dispensation was obtained in December 1367, as the marriage had been deemed uncanonical, because Walter Leslie had previously had illicit intercourse with a lady related within the fourth degree of kindred to Eufamia de Ross. The dispensation is dated at Avignon, viii. Kalend Decembris, anno quinto pontificatus Urbani V., A.D. 1367.‡

Walter de Leslie is a witness to a charter granted by Margaret de Leslie, widow of Sir Norman de Leslie, knight, and confirmed by David II. at Edinburgh, 11th February 1366, to William Cuppyld, her cousin, of the lands of

CHAP. III.
Walter, Earl of Ross.

1365.
1367.

1366.

---
* *Registrum Magni Sigilli*, p. 32, No. 75.
† *Ibid.* p. 53, No. 162.
‡ Stewart's *History of the Stewarts*, Supp., p. 438.

Lumlethyn, Cragoe, and others within the shire of Forfar, and Asdory in the shire of Fife, which belonged to her great-grandfather, Sir Alexander de Lamberton, knight.* David II. granted a charter of the barony of Philorth in Aberdeenshire to Walter de Leslie, knight.† Walter de Leslie, knight, Dominus de Philorth, granted a charter of all the lands which he held in the territory of Monergood, to John Lyon of Terteviot, which charter was confirmed by Andrew de Leslie, Dominus Ejusdem, of whom Sir Walter held these lands, and who in his charter of confirmation calls Sir Walter his uncle. "Sciatis nos vidisse cartam dilecti patrui nostri Walteri de Lesley de Philorth," etc. The charter is dated 1366. Walter de Leslie, Dominus de Ross, granted a charter to Eufamia de Sancto Claro of the lands of Tiry in Buchan, and of Bra, Drum, and Bron, in the shire of Inverness, to be held of him and his heirs by her and her heirs, for payment of two pennies yearly at the feast of St. John the Baptist, if demanded, dated 1367. David II. granted a charter to Sir Walter de Leslie, and Eufamia his spouse, of the lands of the thanage of Aberchirder, and the lands of Blaresnache, to be held of the king for the service of one knight and three suits at three head courts to be held within the shire of Banff; dated

---

* *Registrum Magni Sigilli*, p. 50, No. 151.
† Robertson's *Index of Missing Charters*.

THE FAMILY OF LESLIE.

at Perth, 27th February 1369. King David II. granted another charter of the thanage of the lands of Aberchirder, and of the thanage of Kincardine, to Sir Walter Leslie, knight, with a provision that if the heirs of the old thanes should recover possession, Sir Walter should have the accustomed service and rent paid by them in time past to the Crown; dated at Edinburgh, 6th May 1369. Walter de Leslie, Dominus de Philorth, granted a charter to John de Urchard, son of Adam de Urchard, sheriff of Cromarty, of the lands of Fohesterdy in Buchan, 8th November 1369, which charter was confirmed by David II. 8th November 1369.*

Walter de Leslie, knight, was a member of the convention, held first at Muirhouselow, and afterwards at Roxburgh, 1st September 1367, in the affairs of the Marches, betwixt Thomas, Earl of Warwick, Marischal of England, Lord Percy, and others, on the one part; and Patrick, Earl of March and Moray, Walter, Earl of Douglas, Hugh de Eglington, Walter de Leslie, and others, on the other part. He had a safe-conduct into England on the affairs of David II., 23d January 1368. He is a witness to a charter granted by David II. to William de Dyschyngtoun, knight, at Edinburgh 18th September 1368;† also to a charter granted to Alexander Lindsay, 23d February

---

* *Registrum Magni Sigilli*, p. 63, No. 204.
† *Ibid.* p. 68, No. 231.

1369;* also to a charter, confirming a charter, granted by Thomas, Earl of Angus, Seneschal of Scotland, to Andrew Parker, 15th March 1369.† He was one of the guarantees of the peace with England, 20th July 1369.

David II. granted a charter to William, sixth Earl of Ross, of the earldom of Ross, the lordship of Sky, and all his other lands within the realm, except the lordships and lands which sometime belonged to him by inheritance from Margaret Cumyn, one of the heiresses of Buchan, in the shires of Aberdeen, Dumfries, and Wigton, proceeding on the Earl's free and voluntary resignation of the same in full parliament at Perth, 23d October 1370, to be held by the said Earl and the heirs-male of his body, with remainder to Sir Walter Leslie, knight, and Eufamia, his spouse, and to the longest liver of them two, and to the heirs of the body of the said Eufamia; and if the said heirs were heirs-female, then to the eldest heir-female without division; whom failing, to Johanna, the younger daughter of the said Earl of Ross, and her heirs; dated at Perth 23d October 1370. In the following year, William, Earl of Ross, made a complaint to Robert II., successor of David II., complaining that David II. had given to Sir Walter Leslie, knight, all his lands and tenements, and also those of his brother,

---
* *Registrum Magni Sigilli*, p. 59, No. 184.
† *Ibid.* p. 48, No. 140.

Hugh de Ross, within the district of Buchan, neither the Earl, the complainant, nor his brother Hugh being cited; that he had written to the Bishop of Brechin, then Chancellor of Scotland, Robert, Seneschal of Scotland, Thomas, Earl of Mar, William de Keith, and William de Meldrum, supplicating letters; and also a letter to the king, and to the Lady Eufamia, the complainant's sister; that he had entrusted John de Gairdyn, his chaplain, Canon of Caithness, with these letters; that John of Aberchirder, esquire of the said Sir Walter, met John de Gairdyn and arrested him, and atrociously struck his man because he would not bind his master to his horse's tail, and then robbed the said John de Gairdyn of all his letters and led him to a wood, where he was kept till he paid a ransom, and swore on the holy Gospels, in the presence of Dominus Cristinus, vicar of Forgue, that he would not deliver any of the letters to any one except to Sir Walter Leslie; that the said John de Gairdyn then went and complained to his lord, the Bishop of Aberdeen, and to William de Keith, and then returned to the complainant and related to him what had happened; that the complainant then went in person to the king at Aberdeen, who would not grant his request unless he renounced all his rights in the platan of Forfar into the king's hands in favour of John de Logy; that he made this concession, and was asked to dinner by the king, and

Walter, Earl of Ross.

after dinner asked an answer to his affairs; that a long list of questions was sent to him to answer, containing many authorities from the civil law; that he said that he did not desire any litigation with the king, and had not come for that purpose; that then he returned to Ross without asking leave, and did not speak to the king again till he came to Inverness, when, seeing the king moved against him and his brother Hugh, and the said Walter Leslie to have great influence with the king, and he and his brother Hugh not being restored to the possession of their lands in Buchan, they ratified under their seals the donation of their lands made by the king to the foresaid Walter, on account of greater dangers which they thought imminent; also that the complainant's daughter was espoused to the foresaid Walter altogether against her father's will, who had never made to her any concession or donation of lands or goods up to the time of the death of David II. except through fear of the king's anger. To these complaints, William, Earl of Ross, affixed his seal at Edinburgh 24th June 1371.

William, Earl of Ross, died soon after this, about 1372, and leaving no male issue, he was succeeded in his Earldom and estates by his eldest daughter, Eufamia, Countess of Ross, according to the provisions of the charter of 23d October 1370, and her husband, Walter Leslie, became Earl of Ross in her right.

THE FAMILY OF LESLIE. 73

Walter de Leslie, Dominus de Ross, had a safe-conduct into England 3d January 1373. He resigned the forest called the New Forest in Galloway, in favour of his nephew, James de Lindesay, who got a charter of the same from Robert II., dated at Perth, 20th August 1373.* Robert III., confirmed a grant made by Walter de Leslie to Sir William de Lindesay of the lands of Aberkyrdore and others in Banffshire, 3d October 1373.† Walter de Leslie, Dominus de Ross, had a safe-conduct into England, 20th August 1374, and another, 12th February 1375. Sir Walter Leslie, Dominus de Ross, and Eufamia his wife, granted a charter to his brother-in-law, Sir Alexander Fraser, knight, and Janet Ross, his wife, of the lands of Auchinschogle and Meikle Fyntra in Buchan, and of the lands of Crekiltown, in the lordship of Galloway and shire of Wigton, and of an annual rent of eighteen pounds sterling out of the lands of Farindonald in Ross, in full exchange and compensation for all claim of heritage in the lands of Ross accruing to the said Sir Alexander Fraser and Janet Ross, dated at Aberdeen, 4th June 1375. Walter de Leslie, Dominus de Ross, and Eufamia his spouse, resigned the lands of Balmaledy and Smithyhill, and the lands of Aberluthnot in Kincardineshire, in favour of Patrick de Innerpeffer, burgess of Dundee, who got a

CHAP. III.

Walter, Earl of Ross.

1373.
1374.
1375.

See App. No. XXV.

1375.

---

* *Registrum Magni Sigilli*, p. 99, No. 19.
† *Ibid.* p. 66, No. 139, and p. 160, No. 34.

charter of the same from Robert II., dated at Dundee, 25th December 1378.* Walter de Leslie, Dominus de Ross, had a safe-conduct into England, 14th August 1378.

Walter Leslie, Dominus de Ross, in several charters styles Sir Alexander Lindsay of Glenesk and Sir William Lindsay of Byres "carissimi fratres," his dearest brothers, they being his uterine brothers, sons of his mother, Mary Abernethy, by her second marriage with Sir David Lindsay of Crawford, for which marriage a dispensation was obtained from Pope John XXII. in 1325, and was found in the Vatican by Andrew Stewart.†

In a charter granted by Sir Walter de Leslie, knight, Dominus de Ross, containing a remission of certain services stipulated for in a lost charter, to John Lyon of Terteviot, dated at Edinburgh, 26th December 1375, two of the witnesses are styled Domino Alexandro de Lindesay, domino de Glenesk, et Willelmo de Lindesay, fratribus nostris carissimis. This charter is in the possession of the Earl of Strathmore. In a charter dated at Philorth, 18th August 1381, granted by Walter de Leslie, Dominus de Ross, in favour of Andrew Mercer, of the lands of Faythley and Tyre, in the Barony of Kynedward, and of certain annual rents out of the lands of Findlater, Netherdale, Pettendreich, and Culbirny, in the shire of Banff, two of

---

* *Reg. Mag. Sig.*, p. 152, No. 125, and p. 70, No. iv.
† Stewart's *History of the Stewarts*, p. 446.

the witnesses are designed Dominis Alexandro et Willelmo de Lindesay, fratribus nostris carissimis. This charter was confirmed by Eufamia, Domina de Ross, at her castle of Dingwall, 9th March 1382, after the death of her husband Walter de Leslie.

Walter, Earl of Ross. See App. No. XXVI.

1382.

Walter Leslie, Earl of Ross, had issue by his wife Eufamia, Countess of Ross—

> I. ALEXANDER LESLIE, who succeeded as eighth Earl of Ross at the death of his mother;
> II. LADY MARGARET LESLIE, married to Donald, Lord of the Isles ;
> III. LADY MARY LESLIE, married to Sir David Hamilton.

Walter Leslie, Earl of Ross, died after 18th August 1381, when he granted a charter to Andrew Mercer, and before 9th March 1382, when Eufamia, Domina de Ross, in her pure and legitimate widowhood, confirmed the said charter.

1381.

EUFAMIA,

SEVENTH COUNTESS OF ROSS.

Eufamia, Seventh Countess of Ross.

AFTER the death of Walter Leslie, Earl of Ross, his widow Eufamia, Countess of Ross, married Alexander Stewart, Earl of Buchan, fourth son of King Robert II., and he became Earl of Ross in right of his wife.

Eufamia, Countess of Ross, granted a charter of the lands of Contilech and others to her dear cousin Hugh Munro, ninth Baron of Foulis, dated at Dingwall, 30th April 1379. Eufamia, Countess of Ross, daughter and heiress of the deceased William, Earl of Ross, granted a charter in her widowhood, resigning the superiority of the lands of the western part of Kynfaunys into the king's hands, who granted the same to his nephew, Walter the Seneschal, by a charter dated at Kylwynyne, 24th April 1382.*

Robert II. granted a charter to his son, Alexander Stewart, Earl of Buchan, of the barony of Kynedward, proceeding on the resignation of Eufamia, Domina de Ross, 22d July 1382. He also ratified the donation and concession which Eufamia, Domina de Ross, had made and conceded to his son Alexander the Seneschal, Earl of Buchan, of the earldom of Ross, to be held by him for life, 25th July 1382.† He also granted to his beloved son Alexander the Seneschal, Earl of Buchan, and to Eufamia, Domina de Ross, the thanage of Dingwall, with the castle, on the resignation of the said Eufamia, to be held by the said Alexander and Eufamia, and the longest liver of them two, and the heirs to be legitimately procreate betwixt them, with remainder to the heirs whomsoever of the said Eufamia; dated at Inverness, 24th July 1382.‡ He also granted to his son Alexander the Seneschal, Earl of Buchan, and

---

* *Registrum Magni Sigilli*, p. 166, No. 27.
† *Ibid.* p. 164, No. 20.   ‡ *Ibid.* p. 165, No. 25.

THE FAMILY OF LESLIE.

to Eufamia, Domina de Ross, the baronies or lordships of Sky and Lewes; of the lands in Caithness and Sutherland, Nairn and Inverness, Athole in the shire of Perth; the barony of Fythkill in Fife; all the lands in Galloway; the lands of Forgrundtheny and Kynfaunys in Perth; the thanage of Glendowachy and the lands of Deskford in Banff, which belonged hereditarily to the said Eufamia, and which she had resigned into the king's hands, to be held by the said Alexander and Eufamia, and the longest liver of them two, and the• heirs to be legitimately procreated betwixt them, with remainder to the heirs whomsoever of the said Eufamia; dated at Inverness, 25th July 1382.*

The Countess of Ross does not seem to have been happy in her second marriage; differences arose betwixt her and her husband, Alexander, Earl of Buchan. These differences were brought before the ordinaries of the respective parties, Alexander, Bishop of Moray, and Alexander Bishop of Ross, who, in 1389, pronounced judgment to the effect that the Earl of Buchan should live with his wife, the Countess of Ross, whom he had deserted for Mariota, the daughter of Athyn, and that he should not maltreat the Countess of Ross under a penalty of £200.

Eufamia, Countess of Ross, with the consent

---

* *Registrum Magni Sigilli*, p. 165, No. 26.

of her son and heir, Alexander de Leslie, granted a charter of the lands of Wester Foulis to her cousin Hugh Munro of Foulis, 4th August 1394.

Alexander Stewart, Earl of Buchan, died in 1394, having had no issue by his wife, Eufamia, Countess of Ross, who died soon afterwards, and was succeeded by her son, Alexander Leslie, eighth Earl of Ross.

ALEXANDER LESLIE,

EIGHTH EARL OF ROSS.

ALEXANDER LESLIE, son of Walter Leslie, Earl of Ross, and Eufamia, seventh Countess of Ross, succeeded as eighth Earl of Ross, on the death of his mother, about 1394.

In an agreement made at Calder, 5th September 1394, between Thomas Dunbar, Earl of Murray, and Alexander de Insulis, Dominus de Lochaber, third son of John of the Isles, concerning the possession and superiority of certain lands and privileges, they bound themselves to support each other against every one, except the King, the Earl of Fyff, Malcolm de Dromonde, Earl of Mar, and Alexander de Leslie, heir-apparent to the earldom of Ross.* Alexander de Leslie, Earl of Ross, granted a procuratory of resignation, consti-

---

* *Registrum Moraviense*, p. 355, No. 272.

tuting David, Earl of Crawford, William de Dalziell and John de Ramorgney, knights, his procurators for resigning into the hands of the king, Robert III., all and hail the barony of Fythkill, with its pertinents, in the shire of Fife; dated at Perth, 4th February 1398, and has the Earl's seal appended still entire. The king thereon granted the barony of Fythkill to Sir George de Leslie, knight, of Rothes, and Elizabeth, his spouse, by a charter, 5th February 1398.* Alexander Leslie, Earl of Ross, granted a charter to his beloved cousin George Leslie, knight, Dominus de Rothes, of the lands of Woodfield, Pitnamoon, and others, 8th November 1398, which grant was confirmed by Robert III., by a charter dated at Scone, 4th March 1400, whereby the king confirmed to George Leslie, Dominus de Rothes, the lands of Woodfield, Pitnamoon, the mill of Kincardine, Fettercairn, Eilly, and Bomain, granted to him by Alexander Leslie, Earl of Ross in consideration of his having advanced to the said earl, in his great necessity, the sum of 200 merks to relieve his lands and earldom of Ross out of the hands of the king, the superior thereof, and for his good council and service.

Alexander Leslie, Earl of Ross, married Lady Isabel Stewart, daughter of Robert, Duke of

---

* Original in Rothes charter-room at Leslie House.

Albany, Regent of Scotland, and by her had an only child—

I. EUPHEMIA, who succeeded him as ninth Countess of Ross.

Alexander Leslie, Earl of Ross, died before 1411, and was succeeded by his only child, Euphemia, ninth Countess of Ross. His widow, Lady Isabel Stewart, married Walter, Lord Halyburton of Dirleton.

EUPHEMIA,

NINTH COUNTESS OF ROSS.

EUPHEMIA, only child of Alexander Leslie, Earl of Ross, by his wife, Lady Isabel Stewart, succeeded as ninth Countess of Ross, on the death of her father before 1411.

The Countess Euphemia being under age at her accession, and being, it is said, of a weakly constitution, small, and deformed, was induced by her maternal grandfather, Robert Duke of Albany, then Regent of the kingdom, to resign her rights to the Earldom of Ross in favour of her maternal uncle, John Stewart, Earl of Buchan. Thereupon the Regent granted a charter of the earldom of Ross, the lands of Stroglache, the town of Nairne, with the castle, the barony of Kincardine, the superiority of the barony of Fythkill, and others, to Euphemia, Countess of Ross, with remainder to John Stewart, Earl of Buchan, and his heirs:

THE FAMILY OF LESLIE.   81

whom failing, to Robert Stewart, his brother, and his heirs; whom failing, to the king; dated 15th June 1415. Robert, Duke of Albany, Regent of the kingdom, also granted a charter to his son, John Stewart, Earl of Buchan, of the barony of Kynnedward in the shire of Aberdeen, on the resignation of Euphemia, Countess of Ross, ward.

In order to secure the possession of the earldom of Ross to his son, John Stewart, Earl of Buchan, the Duke of Albany induced Euphemia, Countess of Ross, to take the veil; she became a nun, it is said, in the convent of North Berwick, when the Earl of Buchan took possession of her estates, and assumed the title of Earl of Ross. She died soon afterwards, about 1415, not without suspicion of having been poisoned. On her death the earldom of Ross was claimed by Donald of the Isles, who had married her aunt, Lady Margaret Leslie, daughter of Walter Leslie, Earl of Ross, by his wife, Euphemia, seventh Countess of Ross.

CHAP. III.

Euphemia, Ninth Countess of Ross.

1415.

DONALD, LORD OF THE ISLES;
AND MARGARET LESLIE,
TENTH COUNTESS OF ROSS.

Donald, Lord of the Isles; and Margaret, Tenth Countess of Ross.

LADY MARGARET LESLIE, daughter of Walter Leslie, Earl of Ross, by his wife Euphemia, Countess of Ross, married Donald, Lord of the

VOL. I.   G

Donald, Lord of the Isles; and Margaret, Tenth Countess of Ross.

Isles. When Lady Margaret's niece, Euphemia, Countess of Ross, daughter of her deceased brother, Alexander, Earl of Ross, had declared her intention to take the veil, Donald of the Isles asserted his claim to the earldom of Ross as next heir, in right of his wife, in conformity with the entail made by William, Earl of Ross, her grandfather, in 1370. He disputed the destination made by his wife's niece Euphemia, as being made in prejudice to his wife, who was the lawful heir to the earldom. The Duke of Albany, and his son John Stewart, Earl of Buchan, wishing to keep what they had got, insisted that the resignation of the Countess Euphemia was legal, and they declared that they would maintain it. Whereon Donald resolved to assert his right by force of arms; and he so far took possession that he held the castle of Dingwall, the residence of the Earls of Ross. He raised an army of 10,000 men in the Hebrides and Ross, and marched through Moray into the Garioch, on Mar, intending, it is said, to attack the city of Aberdeen.

Alexander Stewart, Earl of Mar and Lord of the Garioch, the king's lieutenant in the North, collected a body of troops in haste, and met the invader at Harlaw, on the river Urie, about eighteen miles north-west of the city of Aberdeen, 24th July 1411. Although Mar's army was inferior in number, the battle was most obstinately contested, with great loss on both sides. It proved indecisive, however. Both parties claimed the victory. On the side of Donald, the chiefs of Macintosh and Maclean fell, with about 900 men; Mar lost 500 men, besides many persons of rank. Sir Andrew de Leslie, third Baron of Balquhain, who commanded Mar's horse, lost six sons in the battle.

Donald of the Isles was so much weakened by this sanguinary battle, that he was forced to retire, and the Duke of Albany, Regent of the kingdom, shortly afterwards proceeded with a force to the north, and took the castle of Dingwall; and in the following year, 1412, he invaded Donald's territories, and obliged him to abandon his pretensions to the earldom of Ross, and to give hostages for his future observance of peace.

John Stewart, Earl of Buchan, was now styled Earl of Ross, and he held the title till his death at the battle of Verneil, in Normandy, 17th August 1424; and his brother, Sir Robert Stewart, being also killed in the same battle, and neither of them leaving any male issue, the earldom of Ross, in virtue of the limitation in the charter granted to them by their father, the Regent, in 1415, devolved on the crown.

It would appear that although the Stewarts got forcible possession of the earldom of Ross, yet Lady Margaret Leslie did not forego her just claims, and she retained at least the title of Countess of Ross, as is shown by the following document :—

CHAP. III.
Donald, Lord of the Isles; and Margaret, Tenth Countess of Ross.

1420.

"John Byschop of Ross, Dame Margaret of the Ile, Lady of the Yles and of Ross, Huchen Fraser, Lord of Lovat, John Urchard, Lord of Crommathy, Donald of Kalder, Thayne of that Ilke, with many others, till all and sundry, &c. We mak knowyn, truche thir presents that in August 16 year 1420, in the kyrk yharde of Rosmarkyn, compeart Willyam the Grame, son and heyr umquhile of Henry the Grame, in presence of us before a nobil Lord and a michty Thomas Erle of Murreff, his ovyr Lord of the barony of Kerdale, resyngnan over of his auyn fre will in til handes of the sayde Lord the Erle the sayde all his lands of the barony of Kerdale Scheradom of Inverness, and all other lands, to be gyffyn to the sayde Willyam the Grame and his heyris-male, and faylzand them, to Willyam the Hay. Upon the quhylkes thyngis the sayde Willyam the Grame and Willyam the Hay requirit us in witnesyng by our letters testimonial and our seals. The quhilk we grawntit at the place and day before sayde."*

Lady Margaret Leslie, Countess of Ross, had by her husband, Donald, Lord of the Isles, issue—

I. ALEXANDER, who succeeded as Lord of the Isles, and assumed the title of Earl of Ross;
II. MARIOT, married to Alexander Sutherland. She and her husband, Alexander Sutherland, in 1429, got a grant of the lands of Duchall from her brother, Alexander, Lord of the Isles and Earl of Ross.

---

* *Registrum Moraviense*, p. 475, No. 23.

Donald, Lord of the Isles, died before 1427. Margaret, Countess of Ross, and her son, Alexander, Lord of the Isles, were arrested by King James I. when he held a parliament at Inverness, in 1427. The Lord of the Isles was soon released, but his mother, the Countess of Ross, was detained a prisoner, and died about 1429.

ALEXANDER, LORD OF THE ISLES,

ELEVENTH EARL OF ROSS.

ALEXANDER, son of Donald, Lord of the Isles, by Lady Margaret Leslie, tenth Countess of Ross, succeeded his father in 1427, as Lord of the Isles. As has been related, Alexander, Lord of the Isles, and his mother, Margaret, Countess of Ross, were arrested by King James I. when he held a parliament at Inverness in the spring of 1427, because, it is said, that monarch wished to humble the Lord of the Isles, as his predecessors had asserted an independence dangerous to Scotland, and had treated with the Kings of England as sovereign princes. Sir Robert Gordon, in his *Genealogy of the Earls of Sutherland* (p. 67), says King James I. took Alexander, Lord of the Isles, prisoner at Inverness, for manteyning of thieves and not bringing them to justice; but upon promise of amendment, the king soon after did pardon him and set him at liberty.

CHAP. III.
Alexander, Lord of the Isles, Eleventh Earl of Ross.

1429.

Alexander de Yle, Lord of the Isles, granted a charter of the Island of Barra to Gillcowan, son of Roderick Murchard Makneill, 23d June 1427.*

Alexander, Lord of the Isles, raised a body of men in 1429, and besieged the castle and burned the town of Inverness. The king overtook him and defeated him at Lochaber, 23d June 1429. The Lord of the Isles sued for peace, which the king refused to grant. Being reduced to extremities, the Lord of the Isles went disguised to Holyrood on Easter-day, and when the king was at his devotions in the chapel, he fell on his knees before him, and besought pardon and his life for the sake of Him who rose on that day for the salvation of mankind, which the king granted, but sent him to be kept prisoner in the castle of Tantallon, under the Earl of Angus, in order that the islanders might be kept in better subjection. But, notwithstanding this, Donald Ballogh, a brother or near relation of Alexander, Lord of the Isles and Earl of Ross, went with a body of men into Lochaber, and laid waste the country. Alexander, Earl of Mar, and Allan Stewart, Earl of Caithness, proceeded with a force against him; but Donald Ballogh surprised them at Inverlochy, and defeated them, and killed the Earl of Caithness and obliged the Earl of Mar to retreat. Donald Ballogh then returned to the Isles, but, being pursued by the king, he fled to Iceland,

---

* *Registrum Magni Sigilli*, lib. lxiii. No. 152.

THE FAMILY OF LESLIE.

where he was killed, and his head was sent to the king at Stirling, in 1436.*

Alexander de Isle, Comes Rossiæ, granted a precept, dated 24th October 1429, to Alexander Sutherland of Dunbeath, who had married the Earl's sister, Lady Mariot. A free pardon was granted to Alexander, Earl of Ross, in a parliament held at Perth in 1431. After the death of King James I. in 1436, Alexander, Earl of Ross, held the office of Justiciary north of the Forth. In a charter, dated 22d February 1438, in the possession of Innes of Innes, the Earl of Ross is styled "Justiciarius Scotie ex parte boreali aque de Forth." Alexander, Lord of the Isles and Earl of Ross, granted a charter of the lands of Kilravock to John Rose, 22d June 1440.

Alexander, Lord of the Isles and Earl of Ross, married Elizabeth, only daughter of Alexander Seton, Lord of Gordon and Huntly, and had issue—

    I. JOHN, who succeeded him ;
   II. HUGH, whose son Donald succeeded as Lord of the Isles ;
  III. CELESTINE, who had charters, dated 2d February 1463, 8th November 1463, and 10th January 1464, from John, Earl of Ross, Lord of the Isles, his brother. Celestine had a son who died without issue, and three daughters, the eldest of whom, Margaret, married Alexander Macdonell of Glengary, from whom descended the Lords Macdonell and Arros ;
  IV. LADY MARGARET, married to John, eighth Earl of Sutherland ;
   V. LADY FLORENCE, married to Duncan Mackintosh of Mackintosh.

Chapter sidenotes: CHAP. III. Alexander, Lord of the Isles, Eleventh Earl of Ross. 1431. 1436. 1438. 1440.

* Sir R. Gordon's *Genealogy of the Earls of Sutherland*, pp. 67, 68.

Alexander, Lord of the Isles, eleventh Earl of Ross, died about 1448, and was succeeded by his eldest son John, Lord of the Isles, twelfth Earl of Ross.

JOHN, LORD OF THE ISLES,

TWELFTH EARL OF ROSS.

JOHN, eldest son of Alexander, Lord of the Isles, eleventh Earl of Ross, by Elizabeth, daughter of Alexander Seton, Lord of Gordon and Huntly, succeeded as Lord of the Isles and twelfth Earl of Ross, on the death of his father, about 1448.

He was one of the guarantees of a truce with England, in 1449, 1451, 1457, and 1459, and was one of the Wardens of the Marches in 1457. He entered into a confederacy with the Earls of Douglas and Crawford, but he did not engage in the rebellion of the Douglases in 1454. After the death of James II., he entered into a negotiation with King Edward IV. of England, in 1462. A treaty was concluded, 8th February 1462, between Edward IV. and John, Earl of Ross, by which it was agreed that the Earl of Ross, Donald Ballogh, and John de Yle, son and heir-apparent of the said Donald, and all their subjects, and the inhabitants of the earldom of Ross and of the Isles, should become liegemen of Edward IV., do homage, and remain for ever subjects of the kings of England, and assist them against all

THE FAMILY OF LESLIE.

their enemies. King Edward agreed to give to the Earl of Ross, during his life, a yearly pension of 100 merks in time of peace, and of £200 sterling in time of war; and if Scotland should be conquered in consequence of the alliance between them, that part of the kingdom to the north of the Forth was to be given to the Earl of Ross; and in case of a final peace betwixt the two kingdoms, England was not to agree with Scotland, without getting the Earl of Ross and his associates included in the peace.

This agreement was not discovered till 1474, when a treaty being concluded between England and Scotland, and containing a clause that the respective kings should renounce all former engagements, the convention between the King of England and the Lord of the Isles was brought to light. In consequence of this discovery, a summons of treason was executed at the castle of Dingwall, 16th October 1475, against the Earl of Ross, for communing with the king's enemies of England; for leagues and bands made with King Edward; for communing with Sir James of Douglas, sometime Earl of Douglas; for help, counsel, favour, and supply given to the same, and leagues and bands made with him against the king; for giving safe-conducts to the king's enemies of England; for usurpation of the king's authority in making his bastard son a lieutenant to him; for convocation of the lieges, besieging the castle of Rothesay in Bute, and wasting and destroying the lands in Bute. For these offences the Earl of Ross was forfeited in absence in parliament, 1st December 1475, and a force was collected to execute the sentence of confiscation of his possessions. But the earl made his submission, and was rehabilitated in parliament, 10th July 1476. On that day he surrendered to the king the earldom of Ross, the lands of Knapdale and Kintyre, with their pertinents, and the office of Sheriff of Inverness and Nairn, to remain with the crown for ever. The king ratified to Elizabeth, Countess of Ross, spouse of John, Earl of Ross, a grant of the lands of Grenan in Ayrshire, of Kynnedward in Aberdeenshire, of Rew and Ewyl, in the earldom of Ross, granted to her 8th February 1476. He also created John de Isla, Lord of the Isles, formerly Earl of Ross, a baron banrent and lord of parliament; and on the same day the earldom of Ross was inalienably annexed to the crown by Act of Parliament, with power, nevertheless, to the king and his successors to bestow the same on a second son of the royal family.

A charter passed the Great Seal, 15th July 1476, rescinding the forfeiture of the Earl of Ross, and creating him a lord of parliament, and granting to him the lands of Morvarne, Garmorveane, the lordship of Lochaber, Durwan, and Glentoill, in the shire of Inverness; the barony of Kynnedward in the shire of Aberdeen; the lands of Grenan in Carrick, and all the lands which he possessed before his forfeiture, except the earldom of Ross, the lordship of Kintyre, and the office of Sheriff of Inverness and Nairn; to him and the heirs of his body, with remainder to Angus de Ile, his natural son, and to John de Ile, also his natural son. John, Lord of the Isles, had another charter of the foresaid lands, 16th December 1478, to himself and the heirs-male of his body, with remainder to Angus de Ila, his natural son, and the heirs-male of his body; whom failing, to the legitimate heirs of John, Lord of the Isles. This indicates that John de Ile, the other natural son of the Lord of the Isles, was then dead. John de Ila, Lord of the Isles, granted a charter, 22d December 1478, of the barony of Kynnedward, to Alexander Leslie of Wardis; and he had a charter, 11th August 1481, of the lands of Killewnane, and other lands in Kintyre and Knapdale, to him for life.

John, Lord of the Isles, appears now to have returned to his treasonable practices with England. King Edward IV. issued a commission, 22d July 1481, for treating with his dearest cousin, the Lord of the Isles and Earl of Ross, and with his cousins and councillors, and Donald Gorne, for their assistance. These treasonable practices being discovered, the Lord of the Isles was again outlawed and forfeited, as appears from several char-

CHAP. III.
John, Lord of the Isles, Twelfth Earl of Ross.

ters under the Great Seal in 1498, granting to the Macleans of Dowart and Lochbuy, the Macleods of Harris, the Macranalds and Macallans, their lands which they formerly held of the Earl of Ross and Lord of the Isles, and which were then in the king's hands by reason of his forfeiture.

John, Lord of the Isles and Earl of Ross, married Elizabeth, daughter of James, Lord Livingston, great chamberlain of Scotland. She had charters to Elizabeth de Levyngston, wife of John, formerly Earl of Ross, of certain annual rents for the honourable sustentation of her person, dated

1476.   14th December 1476; of the lands of Polquhois, Garreffes, and Garclaithie, in Ayrshire, 29th
1490.   October 1490; and she is mentioned in the
1494.   Records of parliament in 1494. By her the Earl of Ross had no children.

John, Lord of the Isles and Earl of Ross, had no legitimate children, but he had several natural sons, two of whom, Angus and John, have been already mentioned as being included in the remainders in the charters granted to their father in 1476 and 1478. John seems to have died between 1476 and 1478. Angus married Lady Mary Campbell, fifth daughter of Colin, first earl of Argyle, but does not appear to have had any issue by her. But he had a natural son, Donald,
1503.   as it was found in parliament, 5th March 1503, that Lauchlan Maclane of Dowart had been guilty of treason, in the treasonable maintaining, forti-

fying, and supplying of Donald, bastard and unlawful son of umquhile Angus of the Yles, bastard son to umquhile John of the Ilis, in the causing of the said Donald to usurp our sovereign lord's authority, to the effect that the said Donald should be Lord of the Ylis, usurping upon our sovereign lord's authority, and for the causation of our sovereign lord's lieges to obey to the said Donald as Lord of the Ylis, which is our sovereign lord's property, usurping our sovereign lord's authority thereby.

John, Lord of the Isles, twelfth earl of Ross, died in 1498, and was succeeded as Lord of the Isles by his nephew, Donald, the son of Hugh, second son of Alexander, Lord of the Isles, eleventh earl of Ross. The earldom of Ross, as has been related, was forfeited and attached to the crown by act of parliament 10th July 1476.

CHAPTER IV.

THE DISTRICT OF THE GARIOCH.

The Garioch

The Garioch is a fertile district in Aberdeenshire, of which the principal town is Inverurie, situated on a point of land between the rivers Urie and Don, about fifteen miles north-west from Aberdeen. It is bounded on the south by the river Don, which separates it from the district of Mar; on the east and north by Formartine, and the hills of Foundland; and on the west by the river Bogie. It is watered by the rivers Don, Urie, and Gadie, and is overlooked by the beautiful conical hill of Bennachie, which lies in the parishes of Oyne, Premnay, and Chapel of Garioch.

The district of the Garioch was erected into an earldom by Malcolm IV., in favour of his brother David, Earl of Huntington, about 1160. David was succeeded by his son John, Earl of Huntington, in 1219, and he died without issue in 1237, when the earldom of the Garioch fell to his sister Isabel, wife of Robert Bruce, third Lord of Annandale, who was succeeded by her son Robert

1160.

1219.
1237.

Bruce, fourth Lord of Annandale, and father of King Robert Bruce, who, about 1309, granted the earldom of the Garioch to his sister, Christian Bruce, married to his brother-in-law Gratney, eleventh Earl of Mar. Christina Bruce, having survived her son Donald, twelfth Earl of Mar, was succeeded in the earldom of the Garioch by her grandson, Thomas, thirteenth Earl of Mar, who, 1357, obtained a charter of confirmation from David II., of the lordship of the Garioch to be held by him and his heirs whomsoever, as freely as David, Earl of Huntington, had held the same. Thomas, thirteenth Earl of Mar and Lord of the Garioch, died without issue in 1377, and was succeeded by his sister Margaret, Countess of Mar, married to William, Earl of Douglas, by whom she had a daughter, Isabel, Countess of Mar, and Lady of the Garioch.*

PARISH OF CHAPEL OF GARIOCH.

THE parish of Chapel of Garioch is situated in the centre of the district of the Garioch, in Aberdeenshire. The ancient name of the parish was Logy Durno, or Durnoch, which is said to signify a low-lying or hollow place. Before the Reformation there were three places of public worship in the parish—Logy Durno, Fetternear, and a chapel

---

* Douglas's *Peerage*, vol. ii. p. 200.

CHAP. IV.
Parish of Chapel of Garioch.

dedicated to the Blessed Virgin, and called the Chapel of the Blessed Virgin of the Garioch, and which gives the present name to the parish. Early in the seventeenth century the parsonage of Fetternear, lying on the north bank of the river Don, was annexed to that of Logy Durno, on the north side of the Urie. The church was then transferred to the Chapel of the Blessed Virgin of the Garioch, at the east end of Bennachie, on account of its being the most central part of the parish.

The parish of Chapel of Garioch is ten miles in length from north to south, and from two to five miles from east to west. It forms an irregular figure. Its greatest breadth at the northern extremity is five miles, and at the southern extremity three miles, from whence it contracts as it approaches towards the centre of the parish, where its greatest breadth does not exceed two miles. It is bounded on the north by the parishes of Rayne and Daviot; on the east by Bourtrie, Keith-hall, and Inverurie; on the south by Monymusk, and that part of the parish of Kemnay which lies on the south side of the river Don; and on the west by the parish of Oyne and the hill of Bennachie. The rivers Don and Urie flow through the parish. The rocks consist chiefly of granite and whinstone. Cairngorms have occasionally been found of considerable magnitude.

About half-a-mile to the south east of the parish

church is the old castle of Balquhain, long the chief residence of the Leslies, Barons of Balquhain. From it there is one of the finest echoes in Scotland. There is also, at a short distance to the east of it, a Druidical circle, which is very entire. It may be mentioned that there is also a Druidical circle on the farm of Aquhorties, on the Balquhain estate, nearly half way between the castle of Balquhain and Fetterncar House. This circle, one of the most perfect to be found, consists of a large altar stone, and eleven upright stones, which complete the circle. About a mile to the north of the castle of Balquhain, in trenching a piece of barren ground on the Mains of Balquhain, called the Gallow Hill, three human skulls were dug up, which, from the name of the spot, were supposed to have belonged to criminals or vassals in the feudal ages. Also, in 1866, in trenching a piece of barren ground on the farm of Newton of Balquhain, several cairns or tumuli were opened up, and under one of them was found a stone cist or coffin, containing an urn of baked clay full of charred bones. Under the other cairns were found bits of charred bones and charcoal. About half-a-mile to the north-west of the parish church of Chapel of Garioch is a large stone called the Maiden Stone, which stands ten feet above the ground, and is two feet ten inches broad, and about ten inches thick. It is supposed to be sunk about six feet into the ground. It has been en-

CHAP. IV.
Parish of Chapel of Garioch.

graved in the *Sculptured Stones of Scotland*, published by the Spalding Club. It has figures of a warlike kind sculptured on each side. There are various traditions concerning the cause of its erection. The most probable tradition is that which says that it was erected as a monument to commemorate a fray between the Leslies of Balquhain and the Forbesses.

About a mile to the east of the parish church is the battlefield of Harlaw, fought 24th July 1411, between the Royal forces under Alexander Stewart, Earl of Mar, Sir Andrew Leslie, third Baron of Balquhain, who commanded the horse, Sir Alexander Irvine of Drum, and other distinguished leaders, and 10,000 Highlanders and Islesman, under the command of Donald, Lord of the Isles. The battle was long and bloody, and ended in the defeat of the Highlanders, who lost the chiefs of Maclean and Macintosh, and 900 men. On the Royal side the loss was also great, including Sir Alexander Irvine of Drum, Provost Davidson of Aberdeen, and no less than six sons of Sir Andrew Leslie, third Baron of Balquhain. A cross was erected on the place where the Leslies fell, and was called Leslie's Cross from this circumstance.

1411.

The Chapel of the Blessed Virgin of the Garioch was founded at a very early date. Between the years 1338 and 1344, or 1355 and 1357, the sister of King Robert I., Christian of Bruce, Lady of the Garuiach, and widow of Sir Andrew of Mur-

1338-1357.

ray, the Pantler of Scotland, founded a chantry in the Chapel of the Blessed Virgin Mary of the Garuyach, endowing the chaplain, celebrating religious services there for the souls of King Robert, of the founder, and of her husband, with a toft, a croft, containing an acre, in the tenement of Drumdurnach, in the lordship of the Garuyach, and with one hundred shillings sterling yearly from the lands of Meikle Warthill, in the same lordship of the Garuyach.*

In the year 1384, Margaret, Countess of Douglas, Lady of Mar and of the Garuiach, daughter of Donald, third of that name, Earl of Mar, and widow of William, Earl of Douglas, granted a ten-pound land from the two parts of the town of Petgovny, and from the town of Colihill, with the pertinents, excepting the Westfelde, lying in the tenement of Bourty, and the regality of the Garuiach, for the endowment of a chaplain performing the usual religious services in the Chapel of the Blessed Virgin Mary of the Garuiach, for the souls of the founder, of her deceased husband William, Earl of Douglas, Thomas, Earl of Mar, her brother, and James, Earl of Douglas, and Lord of Liddesdale, her son.† Alexander, Earl of Mar, founded another chaplainry in the Chapel of the Blessed Virgin Mary of the Garioch,

---

* *Registrum Episcopatus Aberdonensis*, vol. i. pp. 66, 67.
† *Ibid.* vol. i. p. 167.

and endowed a chaplain who should perform religious services for the souls of those who were slain at the battle of Harlaw in 1411, when he defeated Donald of the Isles. Another chaplainry was founded by Isabel Mortimer, daughter of Bernard Mortimer of Craigievar, and widow of Sir Andrew Leslie, third Baron of Balquhain, for the souls of her six sons slain at Harlaw, and of her husband, who was killed at Braco, 22d January 1420. Another chaplainry was founded by the Leslies of Pitcaple.

King James I. confirmed a grant made by Sir Patrick Ogilvie of Ogilvie, Knight of Grandown, with the consent of the deceased Alexander de Ogilvie, Sheriff of Forfar, his father, to a chaplain performing divine services in the Chapel of the Blessed Virgin Mary of the Garioch, for the soul of Sir Andrew de Leslie, Knight, third Baron of Balquhain, of an annual rent of ten merks from the lands of Strathalva, in the sheriffdom of Banff, failing which, from the baronies of Owchtirous and Essy, in the sheriffdom of Forfar, until he or his heirs should infeft the chaplain in a ten merkland in the Garioch; until which time the presentation of the chaplain should belong to Sir Patrick and his heirs, and thereafter to William Leslie, fourth Baron of Balquhain, and his heirs, 14th April 1425.*

---

* *Antiquities of Shires of Aberdeen and Banff*, vol. iii. p. 269.

THE FAMILY OF LESLIE.

King James III. granted a charter, 28th November 1474, mortifying an annual rent of twelve merks from the lands of Balcomy in Fife, which failing, from the lands of Wardis and Quyltpat, in the sheriffdom of Aberdeen, given by Alexander Leslie, first Baron of Wardis, for the support of a chaplain at the chapel of St. Mary of Garioch, for behoof of the souls of the said Alexander Leslie, and Isabella his spouse.*

King James IV. confirmed a charter, 24th January 1506, granted by Sir Alexander Galloway, chaplain of Collihill, to the Blessed Virgin Mary of the Chapel of Gareauch, and to his successors, chaplains at the Chapel of Collihill, of two acres of land in the barony of Balquhain, for a manse to the chaplains of Collihill; which two acres of land he had bought from William Leslie, fourth Baron of Balquhain, and which he thus disposed of for the praise and glory of God, of the Most Blessed Virgin Mary, mother of God, and of all the Saints, and for the increase of the divine service, and for the benefit of the souls of William Elphinston, Bishop of Aberdeen; Walter Ogilvie of Boyne, Knight; Andrew Elphinston of Selmys; Master Duncan Scherar, Rector of Clatt; William Leslie of Balquhain; and Elizabeth Ogilvie, his spouse.†

CHAP. IV.

Parish of Chapel of Garioch.

1506.

---

* *Antiquities of Shires of Aberdeen and Banff*, vol. iii. p. 405.
† *Ibid.* vol. iii. p. 370.

BALQUHAIN CASTLE.

BALQUHAIN CASTLE, the ancient residence of the family of Leslie, barons of Balquhain, is situated in the district of the Garioch in Aberdeenshire, about three miles north-west of the Royal Burgh of Inverurie, and nineteen miles from the city of Aberdeen. Balquhain Castle stands in a rich valley on the high bank of a small stream. The valley is bounded on the north by a range of fertile heights which extend to the west, and on which is seen the parish church of Chapel of Garioch, built on the site of the ancient chapel of the Blessed Virgin of the Garioch. At some distance on the south is the hill of Middleton, covered with wood. The valley is open to the east, commanding a most extensive view over the varied and highly-cultivated country, through which is seen gliding the river Urie.

The castle of Balquhain was erected at a very early period. George Leslie, first Baron of Balquhain, son of Sir Andrew de Leslie, sixth Lord of Leslie from Bartholomew, the founder of the family in 1067, got from his father the baronies of Balquhain, Braco, Syde, and other lands in 1340, and obtained from King David II. a charter under the Great Seal, erecting the said lands into one free barony, called the barony of

THE FAMILY OF LESLIE. 103

Balquhain. Hence the proprietors of the barony have usually been styled Barons of Balquhain, and the barony has remained in the possession of the Leslie family in the direct descendants of George Leslie, first Baron of Balquhain. The castle of Balquhain appears originally to have consisted of a quadrangular turreted building, having a court enclosed with a wall, and towers on the front. The noble square tower or keep was erected by Sir William Leslie, seventh Baron of Balquhain, about 1530, when he repaired the ancient castle, which had been burned in the memorable feud between the Leslies and the Forbesses in 1526. Sir William made the castle a place of considerable strength, capable of resisting future attacks. It would appear that in the time of Sir William Leslie, ninth Baron of Balquhain, the castle of Balquhain must have been a place of comfort, and even elegance, as the baron, who was then Sheriff of Aberdeenshire, had the honour of entertaining Queen Mary there when she made her progress to the north in 1562. The Queen spent the night at the castle of Balquhain, 9th September 1562, and attended mass in the neighbouring Chapel of the Blessed Virgin of the Garioch.

The castle of Balquhain remained the principal residence of the Barons of Balquhain till the time of Patrick, Count Leslie, fifteenth baron, about 1690. Patrick, Count Leslie, finding the castle

CHAP. IV.

Balquhain Castle.

1530.

1526.

1562.

1690.

of Balquhain incommodious—it having been built more as a place of strength than as a place of residence—removed to the mansion-house of Fetternear, beautifully situated on the banks of the river Don. Henceforth Fetternear became the permanent residence of the Barons of Balquhain. After Patrick, Count Leslie, took up his residence at Fetternear, his son, George Leslie, with his wife, the Honourable Margaret Elphinston, and their family continued to reside at Balquhain Castle, as we find by the *Poll-books of Aberdeenshire*, vol. i. p. 292. On the death of Patrick, Count Leslie, in 1710, his son and successor, George Leslie, sixteenth Baron of Balquhain, left the castle of Balquhain and took up his residence at Fetternear. After this the proud baronial residence was occupied by the factors or managers of the Balquhain estates, and the castle began to fall into decay. It was entirely ruined in 1746. The Duke of Cumberland, while on his way to Culloden, ordered the castle of Balquhain to be burned. There is a local tradition that this calamity was averted by one of the tenants on the estate, John Nicol, who offered the soldiers, sent to set fire to the castle, his broad bonnet full of silver pieces, and said to them, "My lads, I'll gie ye a' this, if ye winna burn the auld place." The soldiers took the money, and filled the vaults of the castle with wet straw, to which they set fire, and when the Duke beheld the dense smoke which enveloped the castle, he was satisfied that his orders had been executed, and he proceeded on his way to Culloden.

The roof of the castle of Balquhain having fallen in through neglect during the disputed succession to the Balquhain estates, after the death of Ernest, Count Leslie, eighteenth baron, people began to pull down the out-wings of the castle, and carried off the stones to build houses and farm-steadings, so that at the present time the large square tower or keep is the only part remaining. No one can behold the crumbling walls of this ancient baronial castle, and the shattered remains of the towering keep still standing erect amid the wreck of so remarkable a building without feelings of regret. There the proud display of the pomp and power of the feudal state long held its sway. The ancient hold, whose former vaulted roof had oft resounded with the joyous sounds of revelry and the social mirth of valorous knights and courtly dames, is now silent as the tomb. The present proprietor, Colonel Charles Leslie, K.H., twenty-sixth Baron of Balquhain, has taken measures to prevent farther dilapidation of the castle. The ground immediately surrounding the castle has been enclosed and laid out in an ornamental manner with plots and evergreens. He is seconded in preserving and ornamenting the place by a most enterprising tenant, Mr. Dean, who has built a handsome residence, and has laid out his garden and the grounds adjoining the castle with great taste.

Several illustrious members of the Leslie family were born in the castle of Balquhain. Among others, Walter, Count Leslie, fourth son of John Leslie, tenth Baron of Balquhain, created a Count of the Holy Roman Empire by the Emperor Ferdinand, who also gave him large possessions in Germany and Bohemia; also James, Count Leslie, eldest son of Alexander Leslie, fourteenth Baron of Balquhain, who succeeded his uncle, Count Walter, in Germany, and was a Field-Marshal in the Imperial service, and held a command in the Imperial army under John Sobieski, King of Poland, in 1683, during the famous siege of Vienna by the Turks; also James Ernest, Count Leslie, eldest son of Patrick, Count Leslie, fifteenth Baron of Balquhain, who succeeded his uncle, James, second Count Leslie in Germany, and was ancestor of the succeeding Counts Leslie.

FETTERNEAR.

THE barony of Fetternear anciently belonged to the See of Aberdeen. It appears that about 1109 a collegiate church was erected at Fetternear, with a foundation for a warder or dean, and canons. Pope Adrian IV., by a bull dated 10th

August 1157, confirmed to Edward, Bishop of Aberdeen, all the lands, churches, and others, granted to the Cathedral Church of Aberdeen by the kings of Scotland; amongst the lands and churches specified in the bull, we find the villa of Fethernear, and the church with its pertinents.* King Malcolm IV., by a charter dated at Stirling 20th August 1163, the eleventh year of his reign, granted and confirmed to the Blessed Virgin Mary, to St. Machar, and to Matthew Kinninmont, Bishop of Aberdeen, numerous lands, places, churches, tithes, and others; amongst others the church of Fetternear, with the lands of the same, and pertinents.† William, parson of Fetternear in 1236, was a witness to an agreement between Andrew, Bishop of Moray, and Gylbert, Bishop of Aberdeen, regarding their jurisdiction over certain charities.‡ King Alexander II., by a charter dated at Kinfawnys 18th September 1242, granted to Ralph de Lambley, eighth Bishop of Aberdeen, the privilege of a free forest in the lands of Brass and Fetternear, so that no one could cut wood or hunt there without the bishop's permission, under a penalty of a fine of £10.§

---

* *Registrum Episcopatus Aberdonensis*, vol. i. p. 6; and *Collections on Shires of Aberdeen and Banff*, p. 145.
† *Registrum Episcopatus Aberdonensis*, vol. i. p. 7.
‡ *Registrum Episcopatus Moraviensis*, p. 101, No. 88; and *Collections on Shires of Aberdeen and Banff*, p. 527, note.
§ *Registrum Episcopatus Aberdonensis*, vol. i. p. 15, and preface, p. xxiii.

CHAP. IV.
Fetternear.

In the Register of the Taxes paid by the Bishops of Scotland, dated 1275, under the head of the Taxes of the churches and benefices of the Bishopric of Aberdeen, in the deanery of Mar, the Church of Fethyrner is rated at iij merks and a half.* Henry le Chen, twelfth Bishop of Aberdeen, granted a charter of the lands of Kyllalchmond, to Patrick de Rothnek, dated at Fetternear on Tuesday after the feast of St. Bartholomew,

1297.
1297.†

Adam Cunningham, seventeenth Bishop of Aberdeen, granted absolution in his chapel at Old

1382.
Rayne, 9th March 1382, to John de Camera, bailie and receiver of the lands of Formartine, and farmer of Formartine, from the sentence of excommunication pronounced against him for not having paid the second tithes for the said lands; and at Fetternear, on the fifteenth day of the same month, the Bishop absolved Robert, the son of Ego, Adam Halde, Angus Faber, and William, the son of John, who all went to Fetternear to obtain absolution.‡

It would appear that the bishop's lands of Fetternear were not always well farmed. The Lords of Council issued a decreet against Thomas Drumbrek, and Agnes his spouse, for labouring

---

* *Registrum Episcopatus Aberdonensis*, vol. ii. p. 52.
† *Ibid.* vol. i. p. 38.
‡ *Ibid.* vol. i. pp. 163, 166.

the lands of Fetternear. The following is a copy of the decreet:—

"At Edinburgh the xiij day of Decembris the yeir of Gode MCCCC,LXXXV yeirs, the Lordis of Consale, decretis and delyueris that Thomas Drumbrek and Agnes his spouss has done wrang in the lawboryng and maunryng of the landis of Fetherner belangin to the bishoprik of Aberdene as wes clerly previt befor the lordis and ordanis thaim to devoide and red the samyn to a reuerend fadir in Gode Wilyhame elect confirmate of Aberdene and that thai·sall content and pay to the sade reuerend fadir the malis and profitis of the sade landis of twa yeirs bigane as he may prufe befor the schereff of the schyr that thai are of vaile togidder with hyis costis and skathis that he hes sustenyt thar throw and ordanis our souerane lordis letteres be derect to the schereff to tak the sade preif befor him and to warne the perty tharto, and the sade Thomas wes lauchfully sommond to this action and oft tymes callit and nocht comperit. Extractum de libro actorum per me Alexandrum Scott rectorem de Wigtone clericum rotulorum et registri ac consilii regis."*

In the rental of the bishoprick of Aberdeen in 1511, containing the tithes of the lands and possessions granted to it by the holy King David, between the rivers Dee and Spey, in the counties

---

* *Registrum Episcopatus Aberdonensis*, vol. i. p. 318.

of Aberdeen and Banff, we find the following entry regarding the lands of Fetternear:—

FETHIRNEYR.

Terra dominicalis iiij aratra gressuma iiij. lib. assedatur pro iiij lib. argenti, iij celdris ordei et, vj. s̃. viij. d̃. pro bondagio cum seruicio. Set quilibet cottarius habens vaccam in dicta villa edificabit vel edificare faciet unam rudam de le fauld pro qualibet vacca. Et tenentes pro tempore respondebunt pro habitatoribus croftorum in hijs que ad agriculturam spectant et de bona proprietate seruanda cum animalibus suis ad ingrassandam terram et alia que ad vicinitatem pertinent. Et si in contrarium factum fuerit in quocumque tenentes respondebunt vt supra.

Johanni Steuin . . iiij. bouate   Willelmo Bisset . . vj. ƀ.
Willelmo Smyth . . iiij. ƀ.   Willelmo Cristesoune ij. ƀ.
Johanni Barcar . . iiij. ƀ.   Willelmo Barcar . iiij. ƀ.
Elizibetht Kow vidue iiij. ƀ.   Alexandro Cristeson iiij. ƀ.

Ortus Palacij.

Assedatur Willelmo Cristesoun pro ij. bollis ordei.

Molendinum eiusdem cum crofto.

Assedatur pro liij. s̃. iiij. d̃. in anno v. bollis ordei quas recipient ab incolis intro scriptis.

Willelmo Smytht   .   . due partes.
Willelmo Matesone .   tertia pars.

Croftagia vj. liƀ. xvj. s̃. iiij. d̃.

Assedantur pro vj. liƀ. xvj. s̃. iiij. d̃. in anno v. bollis ordei vt supra, et x. duodenis gallinis videlicet.

Crofta Mersyntone.

Assedatur pro xij. s̃. in anno vj. gallinis.

Willelmo Smytht.

Crofta Gardiner et Boye.

Assedatur pro x. s̃. iiij. d̃. in anno iiij. gallinis.

Crofta Crag et Kill.

Assedatur pro x. s̃. viij. d̃. in anno et xij. gallinis.

Crofta dicta Crag alias Ellane.

Assedatur pro vj. s̃. viij. d̃. in anno et vj. gallinis.

Crofta Houshil.
Assedatur pro viij. s̃. in anno et xij. gallinis.
Dauid Robertsone.
Crofta Adam.
Assedatur pro viij. s̃. viij. d̃. in anno et xviij. gallinis.
Johanni Steuin.
Crofta Windislie.
Assedatur pro viij. s̃. viij. d̃. in anno et xvj. gallinis.
Jacobo Crommy.
Crofta brasine cum fabrina.
Assedatur pro xxij. s̃. viij. d̃. in anno et xviij. gallinis.
Willelmo Bisset.
Crofta Coy.
Assedatur pro xij. s̃. in anno et xij. gallinis.
Willelmo Cowbane.
Crofta Gilcrist.
Assedatur pro vj. s̃. viij. d̃. in anno et vj. gallinis.
Willelmo Young.
Crofta Mor.
Assedatur pro vj. s̃. viij. d̃. in anno et vj. gallinis.

Crofta Anderson.
Assedatur pro vj. s̃. viij. d. in anno et vj. gallinis.

Crofta Molendini.
Assedatur pro x. s̃. in anno et vj. gallinis.

Kirkhillok et Feriarsett.
Assedatur pro vj. s̃. viij. d. in anno et vj. gallinis.
Alexandro Cristesoune.

Pratum et fenum reseruanter domino quandoquidem a tenentibus eiusdem dominii custodiri debeat ab omnibus suis animalibus et alienis quibuscumque a Pascate vsque ad festum Sancti Michaelis et postquam scissum fuerit fenum predictum arefaciant et in cumulis ponent vt moris est et dominus tantum soluet pro scissura eiusdem.

Carne j. aratrum gressuma iiij. lib. vj. s̃. viij. d̃. assedatur pro iiij. lib. vj. s̃. viij. d̃. in anno j. mutone j. bolla auenarum xij. gallinis et xx. d̃. pro bondagio et seruiciis solitis.

Summa huius dominii in terrarum Firmis xvj. lib. xvj. s̃. viij. d̃.   Summa gallinarum xj. duodene.

CHAP. IV.
Fetternear.

Summa girsume.
Summa bondagiorum viij. s̄. iiij. d̄.
Summa ordei iij. celd̄. vij. b̄.
Summa Mutonum j.
Summa auenarum j. b̄.
Summa aratrorum v.
Piscaria et foresta de Fethirneir reseruanter domino.*

In the same rental we find the following entry:—
"Rectoria de Fethirneir beneficium ad tempus et est de proprietate episcopi."†

1529.

The Rev. Andrew Cullen, parson of Fetternear, son of Provost Cullen of Aberdeen, and also vicar of the church of St. Nicholas in Aberdeen, was a witness to an obligation 14th December 1529, whereby Gilbert Menzies, Provost of Aberdeen, and the bailies of the said burgh, bound themselves to maintain the bridge over the Dee, built by Bishop Gawan.‡

1549.

William Gordon, Bishop of Aberdeen, granted a lease, 7th March 1549, to George, Earl of Huntly, Lord Gordon and Badenoch, Chancellor of Scotland, and Lieutenant of the north, of the barony and shire of Fetternear, with the place of fishing and pertinents of the same, for thirteen years, paying therefor yearly seventeen pounds six shillings and eightpence usual money of Scotland, three chalders, eight bolls of bere, with a peck to every boll, one mutoun, thirteen dozens of poultry, one barrel of salmon for the fishing, or three pounds in money, at the option of the said noble lord, his heirs, subtenants, and helps fore-

---

* *Registrum Episcopatus Aberdonensis*, vol. i. pp. 364-367.
† *Ibid.* p. 380. ‡ *Ibid.* p. 395

said, eight shillings and eightpence for bondage with arrage, carriage, and other due service.*

Soon afterwards the same William Gordon, Bishop of Aberdeen, granted a lease, 22d October 1550, to John Leslie, eighth Baron of Balquhain, of the barony and shire of Fetternear, and of the town of Bonyngtoun lying within the barony of Rayne, for nineteen years, paying therefor yearly seventeen pounds six shillings and eightpence, usual money of Scotland, together with three pounds foresaid for the fishing of the same, or one barrel of salmon at the option of the occupiers, eight shillings and eightpence for bondage, three chalders, eight bolls bere, with one peck to every boll, thirteen dozens of poultry : and for the said lands and town of Bonyngtoun with the pendicles and pertinents thereof, twenty pounds money foresaid, two marts, six mutones, twenty-eight bolls of meal and malt, equally, with a peck to every boll of malt, six dozens of capons, six dozens of poultry, eight bolls of oats with the straw, ten shillings for bondage, with arrage, carriage, and other due service.†

William Leslie, ninth Baron of Balquhain, was Sheriff of Aberdeenshire under the Queen's Lieutenant of the north, the Earl of Huntly. In this capacity he afforded great assistance to the

---

* *Registrum Episcopatus Aberdonensis*, vol. i. p. 447.
† *Ibid.* p. 451.

Bishop of Aberdeen in protecting the cathedral from the ravages of the Reformers, and he supported the bishop in his diocese when all the other bishops in Scotland were persecuted. The bishop, William Gordon, a brother of the Earl of Huntly, as a mark of his gratitude for the services done to him in those perilous times, bestowed on William Leslie, ninth Baron of Balquhain, the barony of Fetternear, with the palace, the tower, and fortalice of the same, with the salmon-fishing in the river Don, and all other pendicles; also the lands of Talzeaucht, lying in the shire of Fetternear: the lands of Bonyngton, with the mill, multures, and crofts of the same: the lands of Lowesk, and the third part of the town and lands of Ledintusche: the lands of Curtestoun, in the shire of Rayne: the lands of Auchlyne, with the mill of the same: the croft of Blairdinny, in the shire of Clatt, with all their pendicles, lying within the county of Aberdeen. The bishop granted to William Leslie a charter of all these lands 8th June 1566, which charter was confirmed by a royal charter 10th May 1602, and by a Papal charter, granted 20th September 1670, by Pope Clement X. to Alexander Abercrombie, who at that time held the barony of Fetternear in wadsett.*

---

* See Charters, Nos. xiv. and xv., Appendix to the Barons of Balquhain.

Mr. Andrew Leslie parson of Fetternear, granted a tack of the parsonage and vicarage teinds of the lands of Fetternear to John Leslie, tenth Baron of Balquhain, for eighteen years, 22d September 1569.* Mr. Walter Gordon, parson and vicar of Fetternear, with the consent of David Cunningham, Bishop of Aberdeen, and of the Dean and Chapter of Aberdeen, granted a tack of the vicarage teinds and teind-sheaves of the lands of Fetternear, to John Leslie, tenth Baron of Balquhain, 18th May 1586.† David Cunningham, Bishop of Aberdeen, granted a charter of the lands of Fetternear and others, to John Leslie, tenth Baron of Balquhain, 5th April 1596.‡ Mr. Alexander Patterson, minister of Chapel of Garioch, was collated to the benefice of Fetternear, 15th August 1606,‖ and the Bishop of Aberdeen issued a commission for resigning the glebe of Fetternear to the said Mr. Alexander Patterson, 13th October 1620.§

About 1621 the parsonage of Fetternear was annexed to that of Logy Durno, on the north side of the river Urie. The church was then transferred to the ancient Chapel of the Blessed Virgin of the Garioch, from which the parish takes its present name of Chapel of Garioch.

John Leslie, eleventh Baron of Balquhain,

---

* Balquhain Charters, No. 512.   † *Ibid.* No. 513.
‡ *Ibid.* No. 458.   ‖ *Ibid.* No. 903.   § *Ibid.* No. 905.

wadsett the lands and barony of Fetternear to his brother-in-law, Sir Alexander Hay of Dalgety, and William Hay his son, for the sum of 11,000 merks, 15th June 1625. Sir Alexander Hay of Dalgety, and William Hay his son, with the consent of John Leslie, eleventh Baron of Balquhain, and Janet Innes his spouse, alienated the lands and barony of Fetternear in favour of Hector Abercrombie of Westhall, second son of Alexander Abercrombie of Birkenlog, by his wife Margaret, daughter of William Leslie ninth Baron of Balquhain, 16th November 1627. Patrick Forbes, Bishop of Aberdeen, with the consent of the Dean and Chapter, granted a charter containing a *novodamus* of the said lands, in favour of Hector Abercrombie, 2d February 1628, which charter was confirmed under the great seal, 29th January 1631. Alexander Abercrombie, eldest son of Hector Abercrombie, succeeded his father in the lands of Fetternear, and as has been related, he obtained a charter from Pope Clement X. 20th September 1670, confirming the same to him.

While the barony of Fetternear was in the possession of the Abercrombies, the mansion-house was attacked by the Earl Marischal's men, as is shown by the following quaint account given by Spalding:—

"The same Sonday (7th June 1640,) about 11 houris at evin, thair cam out of New Aberdein about 200 soldiouris with there commanderis.

At the brig of Done thay divydit in thrie pairtes, quhairof one went in touardis Foveran and Knockhall, another by Whitecarns touardis Wdny, and Fudness, and the 3 touardis Fetterneir. . . These who went to Fetterneir fand the yetis keipit cloiss, the Laird himself being within, and began to persew the entress yet, quhilk was weill defendit, and ane of thir soldiouris schot out thairat, quhairof he deit schortlie thairefter. The rest leaves the persute, and thair hurt soldiour behind thame, and returnis to Aberdein without moir ado. The Laird feiring sum truble to follow, displenishes the place, left nothing tursabill within, cloissis wp the yettis, and took his wyf, children, and servandis with him to sum uthir pairt. But schortlie thair cum fra Abirdein another pairtie of soldiouris to the same place, brak up the yettis and durris, enterit the houssis and chalmeris, brak doun wyndois, bedis, burdis, and left no kynd of plenishing on hewin doun, quhilk did thame little good, albeit skaithful to the owner. Sic as thay culd carie with thame thay took, syne returnit bak to Abirdein ; bot the Laird fled the cuntrie, and to Berwick goes he, suffering this gryt skaith."*

Francis Abercrombie, created Lord Glassford, succeeded his father, Alexander Abercrombie in the possession of Fetternear. From him the

---

* Spalding's *History of the Troubles in Scotland*, vol. i. p. 282.

barony of Fetternear was redeemed by Patrick Count Leslie, fifteenth Baron of Balquhain. Francis Lord Glassford, and Dame Anna Sempill, his spouse, disponed the lands and barony of Fetternear in favour of Patrick, Count Leslie of Balquhain, and Mary Irvine his spouse, and granted a charter of the same to them, in liferent, and to their son, George Leslie, and the other heirs of entail specified, in fee, 20th August 1690.* Alexander Abercrombie of Auchorsk, a member of the Birkenbog family, who rented the mansion-house of Fetternear, renounced his possession of the same in favour of Count Patrick Leslie, 23d August 1690. Since that period the barony of Fetternear has been in the uninterrupted possession of the family of Leslie, Barons of Balquhain.

The mansion-house of Fetternear is beautifully situated in a finely-wooded domain, at a short distance from the bank of the river Don, commanding a view of the river and of the surrounding country. From it are seen in the distance the hill of Corrennie, the hill of Fair, the hill of Bennachie, and others, which form a picturesque boundary to the landscape. The mansion-house of Fetternear was built at a very early period, and was the summer residence of the bishops of Aberdeen. In ancient charters it is styled the

---

* Balquhain Charters, No. 489.

palace, the tower, and fortalice of Fetternear. About 1256, additions were made to the house of Fetternear by Peter de Ramsay, ninth Bishop of Aberdeen, who frequently resided at Fetternear. Other additions were made by Alexander de Kyninmund, thirteenth Bishop of Aberdeen, who completed the Episcopal residences of Aberdeen and Fetternear, and also began to build residences at Mortlach and old Rayne. It is recorded that he was wont, between 1329 and 1341, to pass the winter at Mortlach, the spring in Aberdeen, the summer at Fetternear, and the autumn at Old Rayne, in order that he might more effectually discharge his Episcopal duties in every part of his diocese.

Patrick, Count Leslie, fifteenth Baron of Balquhain, on recovering the barony of Fetternear from the Abercrombies in 1690, found that the mansion-house possessed many advantages as a place of residence, while the ancient castle of Balquhain, which had hitherto been the chief residence of the family, having been built more for strength than convenience, proved less desirable as a residence in more settled times. Therefore he removed from the castle of Balquhain to Fetternear House, which henceforth became the chief seat of the family. At this period the approach to Fetternear House from the south, was through a magnificent avenue of three rows of trees on each side. The mansion-house was very spacious, the front was three storeys high, the windows of the upper storey having pointed tops, with eleven representations of the family arms carved upon them. The house was of considerable length, and had round towers at the east and west end. The tower on the east end had a pepper-box top, with a lofty conical roof; that on the west end was surmounted by a small square house, the corners of which overhung the upper part of the tower. The inside of this small house was composed of one chamber, the access to which was by a narrow stair through the massive wall from the third storey of the main building. There is a tradition that when Sir William Wallace was in the north in 1297, he found refuge in this small chamber, hence the tower on which it was built is called Wallace's Tower. From each end of the main building of the mansion-house there was built a wing at right angles, which thus formed a court, which on the south was enclosed by a low wall surmounted by iron railings, and the entrance to the court was by a large gate opposite to the main entrance to the house. The original building was prepared for defence, which, indeed was necessary in times when the law could do little to secure the tranquillity of the country. There was originally a fosse all round the building, and all the lower chambers, offices, and passages on the ground floor had small windows with iron stanchions, or had long loop-holes to fire through.

THE FAMILY OF LESLIE.

The two towers had also loop-holes, and were ascended by spiral stone staircases. The mansion-house was called the tower and fortalice of Fetternear, and, from being the residence of the Bishop of Aberdeen, it was sometimes called the Palace.

Patrick, Count Leslie, on taking up his residence at Fetternear in 1690, had his arms emblazoned in bold alto-relief on a stone label, six feet long, by four feet wide, with a raised border, and built the stone into the front wall of the mansion-house, above the entrance, where it still remains. Some feet above these arms is a stone with the letters I. H. S. carved on it. The interior of the house was very commodious. All the suites of rooms on the first floor opened into one another, and the long centre room was called the Gallery. Count Patrick Leslie fitted up the mansion-house of Fetternear in a magnificent manner, and furnished and adorned it with a valuable collection of pictures and objects of art which were sent to him from Germany by his uncle, Count Walter Leslie, by his brother, Count James, and by his son, Count James Ernest. Many of these articles had been taken from the Turks, by Count James Leslie, during the siege of Vienna in 1683, and in other battles in which he defeated them. Amongst them were pieces of rich silk and gold and silver brocade stuffs, which were made into church vestments, and some of which still remain at Fetternear. There was also a saddle and bridle with upwards of three hundred pearls on them; a gold-worked sash, a massive gold basin, and several Turkish daggers, highly ornamented with pearls and precious stones.

George Leslie succeeded his father, Count Patrick, as sixteenth Baron of Balquhain in 1710, and died in 1715, leaving two sons who were infants. His widow, the Honourable Margaret Elphinstone, who had charge of the children during their minority, shared in the bitter anti-Catholic spirit of the times, and does not seem to have been zealous for the interests of the family. She resolved to bring up her sons as Protestants, and therefore she sent away from Fetternear all the valuable chapel furniture, and all the Catholic books, and only a very few of these things were ever recovered by the family. Her eldest son, Count James Leslie, died in Paris in 1731, while still in his minority. He was succeeded by his brother, Count Ernest Leslie, eighteenth Baron of Balquhain, who died unmarried in 1739. His mother, who about 1720, had married Sir James Gordon of Park, had persuaded him to leave to her son, James Gordon of Cowbairdy, the lands of Boddam in Insch, part of the entailed barony of Balquhain, and all the household furniture at Fetternear. Thus the family property was dismembered, and all the family heirlooms disappeared, and Fetternear House was stripped of all the relics of former ages which are so highly valued by ancient families.

On the death of Count Ernest Leslie, eighteenth baron, the succession to the Balquhain estates was disputed. A long litigation ensued, and was decided in favour of Count Anthony Leslie, nineteenth Baron of Balquhain, who resided for some time at Fetternear House, but his chief residence was on his family estates in Germany. Some years afterwards, Count Anthony's claim to the possession of the Balquhain estates was challenged by Peter Leslie Grant, on the ground that he was a Papist and an alien. Another long litigation ensued, and after many interlocutors pronounced by the Court of Session, the cause was decided in favour of Peter Leslie Grant, by a decision of the House of Lords in 1762. In consequence of this decision the mansion-house of Fetternear again changed masters. For the first few years, Peter Leslie Grant, being in the Dutch service, came over occasionally from Holland and visited Fetternear. About 1769 he retired from the service, and took up his permanent residence at Fetternear. At this period the mansion-house, though shorn of much of its splendour, was still in a tolerably good state, and the gardens and wooded domains were in perfect order. But Peter Leslie Grant was much pressed for money, and he granted a lease of the whole estate, including the mansion-house and domain of Fetternear, to his agent and relation, David Orme, a lawyer in Edinburgh, for five times nineteen years, at a small annual rent. Peter Leslie Grant died in 1775, and was succeeded by his cousin, Patrick Leslie Duguid, twenty-first Baron of Balquhain, who, with his son, John Leslie, brought an action to reduce the lease granted to David Orme. They succeeded in reducing the lease in as far as it included the mansion-house and domain of Fetternear. David Orme, anticipating this result, did all he could to dilapidate and destroy the place. He ordered all the wood to be cut down, including the ornamental timber and the superb old avenues. Some of the neighbouring gentlemen, anxious to save the ornamental trees from destruction and to preserve them for the family, bought them and left them standing. David Orme insisted that this was a breach of bargain, as the trees were sold under condition of being cut down. He repossessed himself of them, and sold them again for the merest trifle. The fine old gardens, orchards, and shrubberies were destroyed. The two side wings of the mansion-house and the extensive stables and office-houses were allowed to go to ruin, and were then pulled down, and the beams and timber used for firewood. The main building of the house was left in a wretched state. The only relic of family antiquity left was Blairbouy's chair.

This relic, called Blairbouy's, or Jock o' Bennachie's chair, is constructed of massive oak, and is of gigantic size. It is of such weight that the strongest man can hardly lift it from the ground. It derives its name from a stalwart Baron of Balquhain, noted for his gigantic stature, and famous in northern song and legend for his many daring exploits and adventures.

> "His legs were like twa trees o' aik,
> His height was thirty feet and three,
> Atween his brows there was a span,
> Atween his shoulders ells three."

The tremendous strength and dimensions of this chair excite the admiration and wonder of degenerate men of modern days.

John Leslie, twenty-second Baron of Balquhain, on recovering possession of Fetternear from David Orme, took up his residence there, having previously lived at the house of Tullos on the estate of Balquhain, near the foot of Bennachie. His means being limited, he could not undertake to restore the mansion-house of Fetternear to its former grandeur. He contented himself, therefore, with repairing the dilapidations of the main building, so as to render it habitable, and he had the ruins of the two wings cleared away. Thus the features of the place were unavoidably changed, and the venerable antiquity of the mansion-house was lost in its modern shape. The domain, which had been long neglected, or had been broken up into fields and exhausted by overcropping, was put under the best system of modern husbandry to restore it to its pristine vigour, and was then laid down in grass, which at the present time is the finest in that part of the country. Extensive ranges of hills behind the mansion-house were planted, and clumps of trees were interspersed in the domain, so as in some measure to retrieve the desolation which had been made.

In 1818 Mr. Leslie repaired the house of Fetternear, and made some alterations and additions. Unfortunately, the architect employed was allowed to alter the ancient style of the mansion. The small house on one tower and the peaked roof of the other were taken down, as also were the pointed tops with the carved arms above the windows of the upper storey of the main building. These were replaced with battlements not only on the towers, but also along the whole front of the building, and thus the ancient baronial castellated appearance of the house was destroyed. To compensate in some measure for this, a handsome dining-room was included in the additions made to the house. A new approach from the north-east, or Inverurie side, was made through the woods along the bank of the river Don, and it now forms a beautiful drive of two miles up to the house.

Count Ernest Leslie, twenty-third Baron of

Balquhain, did not reside much at Fetternear, but lived chiefly abroad. He was succeeded by his son, John Edward, Count Leslie, twenty-fourth Baron of Balquhain, who, on coming of age in 1841, took up his residence at Fetternear house, which he furnished in a very superior style. He built a new steading of office-houses and handsome lodges at each of the gates, and made other improvements. He was succeeded by his uncle, James Michael Leslie, twenty-fifth Baron of Balquhain, who repaired the old chapel at Fetternear, and made additions to the old chancel, which was the family burial-place, and which he caused to be roofed in, and formed into a vault. He died unmarried, 2d January 1849, and was succeeded by his brother, Colonel Charles Leslie, K.H., twenty-sixth Baron of Balquhain, the present proprietor.

THE PARISH OF LESLIE.

THE parish of Leslie, in the western part of the district of the Garioch, is bounded on the west by the parish of Clatt and by Strathbogie; on the north by the parish of Kennethmont; on the east by the parish of Premnay; and on the south by the Hills of Leslie and the parish of Keig, which separates it from the Valley of Alford.

The parish is very fertile, lying on both sides of the river Gadie, which runs through it from west to east, forming a charming valley. The Gadie abounds in fine trouts, and falls into the river Urie, a little below the Kirk of Oyne. It is celebrated both in Latin and Scotch poetry. Dr. Arthur Johnston of Caskieben wrote—"Crede mihi, toti notus jam Gadius orbi est." and the touching song, "O an' I were where Gadie rins," is well known. There is also a small rivulet or brook called the Burn of Leslie, on the south bank of which the parish church is situated, and at no great distance stands the old castle of Leslie, on the north bank.

At the head of the den of Chapeltown, on the east side of the road leading from Leslie to Alford, there is a place called Little John's Length, or the Four Lords' seat. It is a small circular artificial hollow, about five feet in diameter, and three or four feet deep. Tradition reports that four different proprietors went to that place and dined together, each sitting on his own land. These four proprietors were Lord Glammis, the Lord of Leslie, the Lord of Putachie, and the Bishop of Aberdeen. A little to the west of this place there are vestiges of an intrenched camp, the fosse being yet in several places very distinct; and at a short distance farther west there are a good many cairns or tumuli, one of the largest of which is called Cook's Cairn.

On the south-west of the parish church at Chapelton there was formerly a Catholic church, the ruins of which were dug up many years ago. The baptismal stone font is still to be seen in one of the buildings of a farm-steading. There is a tradition that the farmer who removed the stones lost the whole of his horses, and one race of horses after another, till he was completely ruined, and was obliged to give up the lease of his farm. Here the Leslies of Chapelton had a castle. The Leslies of New Leslie also had a castle about a mile to the north-west of Leslie Castle. So numerous were the Leslies in this locality, that there was a popular song—

> " Thick sit the Leslies on Gadieside,
> On Gadieside,
> The back of Bennachie."

LESLIE CASTLE.

LESLIE Castle, the original baronial seat of the ancient family of Leslie, is situated in a charming valley in the parish of Leslie, in the district of the Garioch, in Aberdeenshire. The castle is now a ruin. It appears to have been a place of some strength. It was surrounded by a fosse and rampart, and had a drawbridge on the west side, protected by a watch tower. It was of the castellated style of building, and consisted of two massive square towers or keeps, joined at right angles, the upper corners of the towers being ornamented with turrets, commonly called pepper-boxes. The walls were for the most part six feet thick. The ground-floor was raised on arches, having vaults underneath. The principal staircase, which is of a peculiar construction, was placed in an angle formed by the two main towers. It consisted of a square tower rising to the whole height of the castle, having in its interior another square tower of smaller dimensions. In the interior, between the walls of the inner and outer towers, was placed the stair, which wound round the inner tower. This inner tower was hollow from bottom to top, having openings like small windows opposite the landing-places of the stair on each floor. It is probable that these openings were for the purpose of calling the servants, because by speaking into one of them the voice is heard from top to bottom. The castle was surrounded by fine gardens, orchards, and ornamental woods, and the hills on the south and south-west were covered with forest.

Leslie Castle was no doubt erected by Bartholomew, the founder of the Leslie family, in whose family the barony of Leslie remained for nine generations, from 1067 till 1439, when it was conveyed to Alexander Leslie, first Baron of Leslie, or of that Ilk, whose family retained possession for eight generations, till about 1620, when George Leslie, eighth baron of that Ilk, mortgaged the barony of Leslie to John Forbes, second son of Forbes of Monymusk. William Forbes, son of this John Forbes, succeeded his father in the barony of Leslie, and he repaired the old castle of Leslie, as appears by an inscription on the wall, dated 17th June 1661. The Forbes coat-of-arms was also placed on the wall of the castle, and over the entrance is an inscription, "Hæc Corp. Sydera mentem."

The barony of Leslie did not remain long in the possession of the Forbesses. It was sold, and is now in the possession of Colonel Leith Hay of Rannes and Leith Hall. The castle of Leslie was inhabited up to the beginning of the present century, when it was occupied by Captain Stewart, agent for the Rannes family. Since then this ancient castle has been allowed to fall into decay; the roof is gone, and the building is fast becoming a ruin. The fosse has been drained, and is now almost filled up. The fine woods which formerly surrounded the castle, and the beautiful ornamental trees, many of them of large size, which ornamented the grounds, have been cut down, and the venerable baronial residence is now a desolate monument of former grandeur.

ROTHES.

THE barony of Rothes, which gave the title to the noble branch of the Leslie family, the Earls of Rothes, continued in the possession of the Leslies, Earls of Rothes, for nearly four hundred years. It was sold by John, ninth Earl of Rothes, in 1711, to John Grant of Elchies, whose grandson, John Grant, Baron of the Exchequer, sold it to James, Earl of Findlater, and it is now in the possession of the Earl of Seafield.

The first mention which we find of the barony of Rothes is in the year 1238, when Eva de Mortach, daughter of Muriel de Polloc, who was daughter of Petrus de Pollock, was Domina, or Lady of Rothes. Petrus de Polloc, grandfather of Eva de Mortach, Lady of Rothes, was witness to a charter granted by William the Lion, 1165-1214, to the church and monks of Kinlos, of the lands of Burgin, lying between Forres and Elgin.* Richard, Bishop of Moray, 1187-1203, confirmed to the abbot and monks of Kinlos, all the grants of lands which they had received from various benefactors. Amongst others, the third part of the Halech of Dundurcus, and the third part of the fishings of the same, which they had received from Petrus de Polloc, to be held by them during the lifetime of the said Petrus de Polloc, after whose death they were to have the whole Halech and the whole fishings of the same. Petrus de Polloc himself is a witness to this charter of confirmation.† Petrus de Polloc is also a witness to a deed regarding the lands of Fither, by William

---

* *Registrum Episcopatus Moraviensis*, p. 454, No. 2.
† *Ibid.* p. 454, No. 3.

the Lion, at Elgin;* also to a charter granted by William the Lion to Richard, Bishop of Moray, 1187-1203;† also to another charter granted by William the Lion to Richard, Bishop of Moray, of certain lands in Banff.‡ Alexander II. granted a charter confirming to the church at Kinlos certain gifts made to it; amongst others, the gift made by Walter Murdach, with the consent of Muriel de Polloc, his spouse, of part of the lands of the Halech of Dundurcus, which formerly belonged to Petrus de Polloc, and which the monks had cultivated with their own hands, and at their own expense, since the death of Petrus de Polloc, dated at Scone, 12th February 1226.§ From this charter it appears thot Muriel de Polloc, daughter of Petrus de Polloc, married Walter Murdach or Mortach before 1226.

Muriel de Polloc, daughter of the deceased Petrus de Polloc, gave to God, to the Blessed Mary, and to the Blessed Nicholas, her lands of Inverokil, for the foundation of the hospital of St. Nicholas at the Bridge of Spey, for the reception of poor travellers. Her charter of these lands is witnessed by Andrew, Bishop of Moray, 1223-1235; Nicholas, Vicar of Rothes; William, brother of Richard, the bishop; and Simon, Vicar of Dun-

---

* *Chartulary of Moray*, p. 6, No. 5.
† *Ibid.* p. 9, No. 11.   ‡ *Ibid.* p. 11, No. 14.
§ *Registrum Episcopatus Moraviensis*, p. 457, No. 5.

durcus.* She made a farther grant to this hospital of the right of a mill and a mill-dam at Inverokil, and also granted some neighbouring lands to the hospital by a charter dated St. Nicholas' Day 1238. Alexander II. granted an annual rent of four merks to the same hospital, for the support of a chaplain, to be paid out of the rents of the mills of Invernairn, by a charter dated at Invercullen 7th October 1232.

A dispute having arisen between the prior of St. Andrews on the one part, and the Bishop of Moray, Lady Muriel de Rothes, and the hospital of St. Nicholas, at the Bridge of Spey, on the other part, regarding the church of Rothes, the matter was submitted to the said Bishop of Moray in 1235. The bishop conceded to the hospital of St. Nicholas the rights which it claimed to have in the church of Rothes, and with the consent of his chapter, and of the foresaid lady of Rothes, he granted an annual rent of three merks, to be paid to the hospital out of the revenues of the church of Rothes.†

By her husband, Walter Murdach, Muriel de Polloc had a daughter, Eva de Mortach, Domina de Rothes, who, for the benefit of her soul, and of the souls of her father and mother, gave to the Blessed Trinity, to the Cathedral Church of Moray,

---

* *Chartulary of Moray*, p. 120, No. 106.
† *Ibid.* p. 123, No. 111.

and to Archibald, Bishop of Moray, and his successors, all her lands of Inverlochtie. She appended her seal to this charter, which is witnessed by Thomas Wiseman, William Duir, Dean of Moray, Archibald Heroc, archdeacon, Henry, chaplain of Rothes, Sir Gilbert de Roule, knight, Sheriff of Elgin, and others, dated Idus Aprilis 1263. She also confirmed to the hospital of St. Nicholas, at the Bridge of Spey, the grant of the church of Rothes, made to it by her mother, Muriel de Polloc. Her charter of confirmation had her seal appended, and was witnessed by William de Aston, canon, Henry, chaplain of Rothes, Robert de Polloc, Ada de Polloc, son of Robert, and others.* Andrew, Bishop of Moray, with the consent of his chapter, confirmed this grant before 1242, in which year he died.†

King Edward I. of England visited Rothes 29th July 1296, on his progress through Scotland, when he received the homage of the Scottish Barons.‡ At Rothes William de Rothenayks swore fealty to Edward, and renounced all leagues which might exist between the Scots and the King of France against the King of England.§

King Robert Bruce granted a charter to Gilbert Wysman of the lands of Rothayes, Auchenboth, Mulben, and Cardeny, between the years

---

* *Chartulary of Moray*, p. 124, No. 112.
† *Ibid.* p. 125, No. 113.
‡ *Ragman's Roll*, pp. 92-100. § *Ibid.* p. 109.

1309 and 1321.* King Robert Bruce also granted a charter to his nephew Randolph, Earl of Moray, son of Thomas Randolph, Great Chamberlain of Scotland, and Lady Isabella Bruce, of all the king's lands in Moray, as they were held by Alexander, King of Scotland, together with all the other adjacent lands contained within the limits and boundaries, beginning at the river Spey where it falls into the sea, and ascending by the same river, comprehending the lands of Fochabers, Rothenayks, Rothes, Boharm, and other lands. This charter is not dated, but is supposed to have been granted about 1312.†

In 1390 we find Sir George Leslie, grandson of Sir Andrew Leslie, VI. Dominus Ejusdem, styled Dominus de Rothes. Sir George Leslie, Dominus de Rothes, is a witness to a contract of marriage, 26th April 1392, as has been related in the records of the Rothes family, but it has not been ascertained how he obtained possession of the barony of Rothes.

Mr. Andrew Leslie, chaplain of the chapel of the Blessed Virgin Mary within the castle of Rothes, with the consent of George, Earl of Rothes, patron of the said chapel, and of Patrick, Bishop of Aberdeen, and of the chapter of the said diocese, granted a feu-charter of all and haill the

---

* Robertson's *Index*, No. 57.
† *Registrum Moraviense*, p. 342, No. 264.

lands of Chapel Hill, with its pertinents, belonging to the said chapel, lying within the lordship of Rothes and shire of Moray, in favour of George Leslie, son and heir-apparent of an honourable man, William Leslie of Culclaraquhey. A precept of sasine followed thereon, dated 1555, and is signed only by the chaplain, and his seal only is affixed, though it bears to have the earl's and the bishop's seals adhibited.

Mr. James Leslie, chaplain of the chaplainry of Rothes, granted a tack of the lands of Chapel Hill of Rothes, and of the teinds of the same, and of the lands of Dandaleith, pertaining to him as part of the patrimony of the said chaplainry, to Andrew, Earl of Rothes, for the space of three years from Whitsunday 1571.

In the rental of the diocese of Moray for the terms of Whitsunday and Martimas 1565, we find that the church lands of Rothes were valued at forty-six shillings and eightpence, one quarter of a mart, one sheep, one lamb or kid, one dozen capons, one boll oats with straw, and fourteen shillings for six firlots of meal.*

In Shaw's *History of Moray* we find the following account of the parish of Rothes :—

"The parish of Rothes in Erse is called Rauis or Raudh-uis, that is, red water, from the red banks of the river and brooks. It extendeth on

---

* *Registrum Moraviense*, p. 440.

the river-side in a beautiful plain from north-north-east to south-south-west, about two miles; and in the lower end a defile called the glen of Rothes, stretcheth among the hills towards Elgin, three miles to the north-north-west. The church standeth upon the side of a brook, a quarter of a mile from the river, and half-a-mile from the north end of the parish; one mile south of Dundurcos Church, three miles north of Aberlour, and about five miles north-east of Knockando. In the year 1238 Eva de Mortach was Domina de Rothes. In the reign of King Alexander III., Norman Lesly of Lesly in the Garioch, married the daughter and heiress, it is said, of Watson of Rothes, and from that time the barony continued to be the property of the family of Leslie till the beginning of this century (the eighteenth). Captain John Grant of Easter Elchies made a purchase of it, and his grandson, John Grant, Baron of Exchequer, sold the barony of Rothes, and the baronies of Easter Elchies and Edinville, anno 1758, to James, Earl of Findlater. The east side of the glen of Rothes pertaineth in feu-holding to Robert Innis of Blackhills, and the west side is the feu property of Robert Cumming of Loggie. Near the church stood the castle or fortalice of Rothes, which carries the mark of an ancient building. It stood on a green mount, surrounded by a dry ditch or fosse, and is now in ruins. The whole of the parish is in the county of Elgin or Moray."

THE FAMILY OF LESLIE.

The parish of Rothes was extended in 1782 by the annexation of part of the parish of Dundurcos, and the following account of the state of the parish in 1825 is given in a note appended to Shaw's description :—

"The parish of Rothes in its present extent, along the western bank of the Spey, measures nearly ten miles from the lower Craigelachy to the boundary of the parish of Speymouth, upon the Duke of Gordon's estate of Dipple. The mountain receding in its bendings from the river, has shaped the parish into four beautiful extensive plains of Dunnaleith, Rothes, Dundurcos, and Ortown. Many farms also stretch backward on the more gentle declivities of the mountain : and in the valleys along the sundry brooks sent forth from the mountain through those plains into the river. Rothes comprehends also the peninsula of Akaunwall, part of the estate of Arndilly, projected in a promontory form from the bottom of the mountain of Bennegin, insulated on all its sides by the winding of the river. There is the defile also of the glen of Rothes, opening northward quite through the mountain into the broad champagne of Moray, containing the estate of Auchnaroth, the property of William Robertson, Esq. ; and the glens with Pitcraiggy, appertaining to the family of Cumming of Loggie. Auchnaroth exhibits a handsome dwelling, with the requisite embellishments of groves, gardens, and extensive

CHAP. IV.
Rothes.

plantations, with a large extent of the mountain backward, for the production of grouse, and the maintenance of sheep. Ortown House, the property of Richard Wharton Duff, Esq., is the only family seat. An extensive plain of fertile corn-fields spread backwards more than a mile from the river. A wood-clothed bank sweeps circular along the other side, presenting near its margin above an inviting elevated situation for the house—a modern, large, elegant building of four storeys, with appropriate wings, containing a suite of magnificent public rooms. The paintings, though pretty numerous, are, in general, family and other portraits. There are a few specimens of the polygraphic art, landscapes little distinguishable from common paintings. The library is a lofty and spacious room, fitted up in an elegant and commodious style. The approach is judiciously opened through a sheltering grove, with its ornamental shrubbery continued along the green lawn, which spreads around the house. Within the recess of a grove, on the plain under the wood-clothed bank, is the spacious orchard, in contiguity with an extensive garden, with a long range of hot-house, rearing the pine-apple and the grape; besides a large extent of brick-lined wall for the more delicate kinds of European fruitage. The bank presents an inviting shade and shelter to the circumjacent fields, and an indefinite extent of forest, fir, larix, and all the variety of deciduous trees, clothe the face of the mountain behind. On one prominent intermediate height a neat modern watch-tower commands the landscape; the winding course of the broad rolling river—Gordon Castle, and its decorated domain—the whole of the varied plain on the north—and a great extent of the sea. In the year 1776 a village was begun by the Earl of Seafield, on the plain of Rothes, upon leases of thirty-eight years, and the liferent thereafter of the possessor, after which the building might be purchased by the landlord. Each tenement is the eighth part of an acre of Scots measure, at the rent of ten shillings yearly. From one half to two acres of land at an adequate rent is occupied with each tenement without the security of a lease. The village accommodates nearly 400 inhabitants. The establishment of no manufactory has yet been proposed, though a considerable stream working a corn-mill, a carding-mill, and a fulling-mill, runs behind the gardens. The exigencies of the country are supplied by the requisite artisans."*

Shaw gives the following ecclesiastical history of the parish of Rothes :—

"Rothes was a parsonage, the Earl of Rothes patron, but now the Earl of Findlater. The stipend is 40 bolls of oat-meal, and 370 merks, without allowance for communion elements, and

---

* Shaw's *History of Moray*, p. 20.

CHAP. IV.
Rothes.

1576.

1620.

without a decreet of modification. The salary of the school is not legal. The catechisable persons are 500. No mortifications. The inscription on the gravestone of Mr. James Leslie runneth thus. 'Here lies ane nobleman, Mr. James Lesly, parson of Rothes, brother-german to George, umquhile Earl of the same, who departed in the Lord, 13th October 1576.' To him succeeded Mr. Alexander Lesly, whose successor was Mr. Leonard Leslie. In a discharge granted by the Earl of Rothes to one Margaret Anderson, dated at the castle of Rothes, anno 1620, Mr. Leonard Lesly is a witness; the ministers are—

"Mr. JAMES LESLEY, Exhorter and parson 1570, died October 13, 1576.
ALEXANDER LESLEY, died about 1610.
LEONARD LESLEY, parson in 1620.
JOHN WEMYS, brother to Lord Wemys, ordained June 1, 1622, died February 25, 1640.
ROBERT TOD, ordained May 5, 1642, Transported to Urquhart 1662.
JOHN LESLEY, ordained November 4, 1663, died about 1692.
JAMES ALLAN, ordained September 23, 1696, deposed for Burroignionism, May 29, 1706.
GEORGE LINDSAY, ordained August 22, 1710, transported to Aberlowe, 1714.
ALEXANDER TOD, ordained November 11, 1714, died April 11, 1716.
THOMAS FAIRBAIRN, ordained in 1717, transported to Gartlie 1719.
JOHN PAUL, ordained November 10, 1720, died March 16, 1747.
JAMES GRAY, ordained April 1714, transported to Lanark, 1755.

ALEXANDER PATERSON, ordained in 1759, admitted July 17, 1760, transported to Cullen 1762.
JAMES OGILVIE, from Ordequhill, admitted March 24, 1763.
GEORGE CRUICKSHANKS, admitted September 25 1788."*

* Shaw's *History of Moray*, p. 363.

APPENDIX.

APPENDIX No. I.

II. MALCOLM.

CHARTER granted by DAVID, Earl of Huntingdon, brother of King William the Lion, to MALCOLM, the son of BERTOLF, of the Lands of Leslie and others—1171-1199.

DAVID frater Regis Scocie omnibus probis hominibus tocius terre sue clericis et laicis . Francis et Anglis . Flamingis et Scotis tam presentibus quam futuris . Salutem . Sciatis me dedisse et concessisse et hac carta mea confirmasse Malcolmo filio Bartholf et heredibus suis terram suam in Lesslyn sicut perambulata fuit ei coram M (Mattheo) Episcopo de Abirden et per probos homines meos . et Hachennegort per rectas divisas suas . et Mache per rectas divisas suas . cum omnibus justis pertinenciis suis et libertatibus in bosco et plano in terris et agris in pratis et pascuis in moris et mossis et maresiis in ecclesiis et capellis in molendinis et stagnis in vivariis et piscariis et omnibus aliis aysiamentis tam non nominatis quam nominatis . Tenendas sibi et heredibus suis de me et heredibus meis in feodo et hereditate libere et quiete et honorifice cum sacca et socco cum tholl et them et infangandthef cum furca et omnibus aliis libertatibus praeter fossam . per servitium unius militis.

Testibus .

M (Mattheo) Episcopo de Abirden.
Malcolmo filio Comitis Anegus.
(Duncan) filio Brouiss judice.
R(oberto) de Kerneil.
Herberto de Arches (Archel).
Allano filio Hugonis.
Waltero de Bosyth (Bisset).
Gilleberto de Lancas (Lacu).
Nicalao de Aelles (Adles).
Willelmo de Vaial (Wacet).

Original in Charter-room of the Earls of Rothes at Leslie House.

APPENDIX No. II.

II. MALCOLM.

CHARTER by DAVID, Earl of Huntingdon, to the Abbey of Arbroath, witnessed by MALCOLM, the son of BERTOLF.

DAVID frater Regis Scotorum . omnibus . &c. Sciatis me dedisse &c. Deo et ecclesie Sancti Thome de Arbrothe et Monachis ibidem Deo servientibus pro animabus patris et matris mei &c. et pro anima mea et pro anima Matilde sponse mee unam carucatam terre in Kinalchmund &c. in piam et perpetuam elemosinam . &c. his testibus
>Willelmo rege Scotorum fratre meo.
>H. (Henrico) filio meo (Henry of Brechin).
>MALCOLMO FILIO BERTOLF (LESLIE).
>Recardo Capellano meo.
>Phillippo Clerico meo et aliis.

Registrum vetus Cenobii de Aberbrothie, p. 624.

APPENDIX No. III.

III. NORMAN.

CHARTER by JOHN, Earl of Huntingdon, to NORMAN, the son of MALCOLM, of the Lands of Lesselyn, Achnagart, Mile, and Caskyben, etc.—1219-1237.

OMNIBUS hoc scriptum visuris vel audituris Joannes Comes de Huntingtoun salutem. Noveritis me concessisse et hac presenti carta mea confirmasse Normanno filio Malcolmi terram de Lesselyn et Achnagart et Mile tenendam sibi et heredibus suis de me et heredibus meis in feodo et hereditate per suas rectas divisas cum omnibus pertinenciis et libertatibus suis sicut carta patris mei quam inde habet testatur excepta donacione Ecclesie de Lesselyn quam dictus Normannus dedit Abbacie de Lundores et monachis ibidem Deo servientibus sicut carta ipsius Normanni quam idem Monachi inde habent testatur . Dedi etiam et concessi eidem Normanno et heredibus suis totam terram de Caskyben per suas rectas divisas et cum omnibus pertinenciis suis ad incrementum praedictarum terrarum . Faciendo inde mihi et heredibus meis pro omnibus prenominatis terris servicium feodi unius militis . Hisce testibus . Domino Johanne tunc Abbate de Lindoris . Henrico de Brechin . et Henrico de Strivelyn . fratribus meis . Roberto de Campania . Henrico de Frevill . Johanne de Bruiss . Henrico de Boysuill . David de Andrus . et Willelmo de Cull.

APPENDIX. III.

Original in Charter-room of the Earls of Rothes at Leslie House.

APPENDIX No. IV.

III. NORMAN.

Appendix IV.

CHARTER by MATTHEW KINNINMOUNT, Bishop of Aberdeen, for the erection of St. Peter's Hospital, in the Spittal, near Aberdeen, witnessed by NORMAN, the Constable of Inverurie—1165-1169.

UNIVERSIS Sancte Matris ecclesie filiis Matheus Dei gracia Aberdonensis ecclesie minister humilis . Salutem in Christo . Sciant tam presentes quam futuri nos divina inspirante gracia pro anima regis Willelmi et pro animabus antecessorum et successorum suorum et pro anima nostra et pro animabus antecessorum et successorum nostrorum Hospitale infirmorum fratrum statuisse in honorem Beati Petri Apostolorum Principis in territorio de Aberden et eidem Hospitali et infirmis ibidem commorantibus terram quae dicitur Ardschelly et Petenderleyn . Carnahard et Ardonachyn per rectas divisas suas excepta terra illa quam Caperoni homini nostro dedimus et ei per divisas assignavimus dedisse concessisse et hac carta mea confirmasse in liberam et perpetuam eleemosynam cum terra illa que est

APPENDIX IV.

circa ipsum hospitale et cum omnibus decimis dominii nostri de Aberdeyn preter illas decimas quas clericis ecclesie Sancte Marie servientibus in perpetuum assignavimus . Concedimus eciam eisdem infirmis decimam cani nostri et placitorum nostrorum atque lucrorum et decimam firme nostre tam in farina quam brasio et prebenda . decimam quoque frumenti nostri . salis et ferri . carnium quoque et piscium omniumque cibariorum que in domo nostra expendunter . Quare volumus ut prefatum hospitale et infirmi ibidem manentes terras et omnes decimas prenominatas et omnes possessiones suas ita libere et quiete teneant et possideant sicuti aliqua domus fratrum infirmorum in regno Scocie constituta liberius et quiecius tenet et possidet . Testibus Simone archidiacono nostro . Roberto decano . Magistro Matheo . Willelmo . Galtero . Bricio Capellanis nostris . Willelmo persona . Matheo Senescallo nostro . Thoma nepote nostro . Joanne filio Archid . Mauricio persona de Tarves . Gillochero comite de Mar . Fergo comite de Buchan . Malcolmo . Jacobo filiis Morgundi . NORMANO CONSTAPULARIO DE ENNROURY . Baldueno clerico . Roberto de Raij . Willelmo de Tatenhill . Willelmo de Slanes milite . Dunecano Makfety . Willelmo filio Hugonis . Gilberto filio Roselini.

Collections for a History of the Shires of Aberdeen and Banff; Spalding Club, pp. 153, 154.

Appendix V.

1202-6.

APPENDIX No. V.

III. NORMAN.

CHARTER of the Foundation of the Church and Abbey of Lindores by DAVID, Earl of Huntingdon, witnessed by NORMAN, the son of MALCOLM, and Constable of Inverurie—1202-1206.

UNIVERSIS Sancte Matris ecclesie filiis et fidelibus tam presentibus quam futuris Comes David frater regis

Scocie salutem . Sciatis me fundasse quandam Abbaciam apud Lindors de ordine Kelchoensi ad honorem Dei et Sancte Marie virginis et Sancti Andree Apostoli omniumque Sanctorum pro salute anime David regis avi mei et pro salute anime comitis Henrici patris mei et comitisse Ade matris mee et Malcolmi Regis fratris mei et pro salute anime regis Willelmi fratris mei et regine Armegard et omnium antecessorum meorum et pro salute anime mee et Matildis comitisse sponse mee et pro salute anime David filii mei et omnium successorum meorum et pro salute animarum fratrum et sororum mearum Concessi eciam et hac carta mea confirmavi predicte Abbacie de Lindors et monachis ibidem Deo servientibus in liberam et puram et perpetuam elemosinam ecclesiam de Lindors cum omnibus pertinenciis suis et terram ad predictam ecclesiam pertinentem in bosco et plano sicut eam Magister Thomas tenuit et habuit . et ecclesiam de Dunde cum omnibus pertinenciis suis . et ecclesiam de Fintrith cum omnibus pertinenciis suis . et ecclesiam de Inverurin cum capella de Munkegin et cum omnibus aliis pertinenciis suis . et ecclesiam de Durnach et ecclesiam de Prame . et ecclesiam de Radmuriel . et ecclesiam de Inchemabanim . et ecclesiam de Culsamuel . et ecclesiam de Kelalcmund . cum capellis earundem ecclesiarum et terris et decimis et omnibus aliis pertinenciis earum . ad proprios usus et sustentaciones eorundem monachorum . Quare volo et concedo ut predicti monachi habeant et teneant in perpetuam et puram elemosinam predictas ecclesias cum capellis et terris et decimis et omnibus aliis pertinenciis suis sine omni servicio et consuetudine et auxilio seculari et exaccione bene et in pace libere quiete plenarie integre et honorifice sicut aliqua Abbacia vel domus religionis in toto regno Scocie melius liberius quiecius plenius et honorificencius aliquas ecclesias vel aliquas alias elemosinas habet et possidet . Has autem ecclesias prenominato monasterio de Lindors et monachis ibidem Deo servientibus ita libere et pacifice jure perpetuo possidendas concessi et confirmavi ut mihi succedencium nullus aliquid ab eis nisi solas oraciones ad anime salutem exigere pre-

APPENDIX V.

APPENDIX V.

sumat . His testibus Willelmo Rege Scocie . Johanne Episcopo Aberdonensi . Radulfo Episcopo Brehinensi . Osberto Abbate Kelchoensi . Henrico Abbate de Aberbrudoc . Simone Archidiacono de Aberdoen . Roberto decano de Aberdoen . Waltero officiali . Matheo de Aberdoen . clerico domini Regis . David de Lindeseia . Waltero Olifard . Roberto Basset . Walkelino filio Stephani . Willelmo Wascelin . Galfrido de Watervile . NORMANO FILIO MALCOMI . CONSTABULARIO DE INVERURIN . Henrico de Bevile . Matheo falconario . Simone Flamang . cum aliis multis.

Denmylne Collection of Charters, MSS., Advocates' Library, Edinburgh ; and *Collection for Shires of Aberdeen and Banff*, pp. 246, 247, Spalding Club.

Appendix VI.

APPENDIX No. VI.

IV. NORINO.

CHARTER granted by King ALEXANDER II. to NORINO, son of NORMAN, of the Lands of Leslie in Free Forest—A.D. 1248.

1248.

Alexander Dei Gratia Rex Scotorum omnibus probis hominibus terre sue Salutem . Sciatis nos ad instanciam Isobile de Bruiss et Roberti de Bruiss filii sui concessisse Norino filio Normanni constabulario tenenti suo ut terram suam de Lesslyn et Boscum suum de Lesslyn quas de eis tenet habeat in liberam forestam . Quare firmiter prohibemus ne quis in dicto bosco sine ejus licencia speciali secet aut venetur super nostram plenariam forisfacturam decem librarum . Testibus Willelmo Comite de Mar . Alexandro filio Walteri Senescallo . Joanne Cumyn et Nicolao de Soulis . Apud Edinburg quarto die mensis Decembris . anno regni nostri tricesimo quarto (viz. 4th December 1248).

Original Charter in Charter-room of the Earls of Rothes at Leslie House.

APPENDIX No. VII.

VIII. SIR ANDREW DE LESLIE, DOMINUS EJUSDEM.

COPY of a DISCHARGE by Sir ANDREW DE LESLIE, VIII. Dominus Ejusdem, to Sir THOMAS HAY, Lord Errol, for £200 sterling.

PATEAT universis per presentes me Andream de Lesley Dominus Ejusdem recepisse et plenarie habuisse per manus Thomae de Haia Domini de Errol Constabularii de Scocie ducentos libros bonorum et legalium sterlingorum . In quibus idem Thomas de Haia ratione cujusdam contractus super matrimonium inter filium meum et filiam suam habendum mihi liberatorie extitit obligat . de quorum quidem ducentorum librorum pecunie solutione et receptione habeo me contentum . In cujus rei testimonium presentibus sigillum meum apposui apud Dunde duodecimo die Julii Anno Domini M°c.c.c. lxx° sexto (*i.e.* 12th July 1376). 1376.

Original in Charter-room of the Earl of Errol.

APPENDIX No. VIII.

VIII. SIR ANDREW DE LESLIE, DOMINUS EJUSDEM.

CHARTER granted by King ROBERT III., in favour of NORMAN DE LESLIE and Sir GEORGE LESLIE of Rothes—18th August 1390. 1390.

ROBERTUS Dei gratia Rex Scottorum omnibus probis hominibus tocius terre sue clericis et laicis salutem . Sciatis nos dedisse concessisse et hac presenti carta nostra confirmasse Normano de Lessley terras baronie de Balnebrech infra vicecomitatum de Fyff et terras baronie de Lour et terras de Dunlopy infra vicecomitatum de Fforfar terras eciam baroniarum de Cusschene et Rothynor-

APPENDIX VIII.

mane cum pertinenciis infra vicecomitatum de Abyrdene que fuerunt dicti Normani et quas ipse non vi aut metu ductus nec errore lapsus sed sua mera et spontanea voluntate per fustum et baculum per terras suas resignacionis sursum reddidit pureque et simpliciter resignavit in manibus excellentissimi principis quondam domini Roberti Dei gratia Regis Scottorum illustris nostri progenitoris apud Linlithgow in ultimo consilio suo ibidem tento ac totum jus et clameum que in dictis terris cum pertinenciis habuit aut habere potuit pro se et heredibus suis omnino quittum clamavit imperpetuum . Tenendas et habendas eidem Normano et heredibus suis masculis de corpore suo legitime procreatis seu procreandis et ipsis forte deficientibus Georgio de Lessley militi et heredibus suis masculis de corpore suo legitime procreandis et ipsis deficientibus heredibus dicti Normani legitimis quibuscumque in feodo et hereditate per omnes rectas metas et divisas suas cum omnibus et singulis libertatibus commoditatibus aysiamentis et justis pertinenciis quibuscumque ad dictas terras spectantibus seu juste spectare valentibus quomodolibet infuturum . faciendo inde nobis et heredibus nostris servicia debita et consueta reservato tamen Andree de Lessley patri dicti Normani pro toto tempore vite sue libero tenemento terrarum omnium predictarum cum pertinenciis . In cujus rei testimonium presenti carte nostre nostrum precipimus apponi Sigillum Testibus venerabilibus in Christo patribus Waltero et Matheo Sancti Andree et Glasguensis ecclesiarum Episcopis . Roberto de Fif et de Meneteth fratre nostro dilecto . Archebaldo de Douglas domino Galwidie . Comitibus Jacobo de Douglas domino de Dalketh . Thoma de Erskyne consanguineis nostris dilectis militibus et Alexandro de Cockburn de Langton custode magni sigilli nostri . Apud Sconam octodecimo die Augusti tempore coronacionis nostre ibidem celebrate . Anno regni nostri primo (*i.e.* 18th August 1390).

1390.

Registrum Magni Sigilli, p. 187, No. 17.

APPENDIX No. IX.

VIII. Sir Andrew de Leslie, Dominus Ejusdem.

Charter granted by Sir Andrew de Leslie, VIII. Dominus Ejusdem, to his Brother-in-law, David de Abercrombie, and Margaret de Leslie his Spouse— 30th May 1391.

Omnibus &c—Andreas de Lesley Dominus Ejusdem salutem. Noveritis me cum consensu et assensu Domini Normani de Lesley militis filii mei et heredis dedisse et per hanc cartam meam confirmasse David de Abercromby et Margarite sponse sue sorori mee carissime in libero maritagio omnes et singulas terras meas de Achquhorthy de Acquhorsk et de Blairdaff cum pertinenciis suis jacentes in regalitate de Garvyach infra vicecomitatum de Aberdene. Tenendas &c. prefatis David et Margarita ac eorum diutius vivente heredibusque inter ipsis legitime procreatis seu procreandis quibus forte deficientibus mihi et heredibus meis quibuscumque in feodo, &c . . . de me et heredibus meis dominis de Lesley imperpetuum per omnes rectas metas et cum bondis bondagiis nativis et locum sequelis &c. Faciendo inde mihi et heredibus meis dominis de Lesley sectam communem ad curias nostras tenendas infra baroniam de Lesley. Volo tamen quod omnes tenentes et singuli qui inhabitaverint terras meas de Lesley capiant et habeant miremia sibi necessaria ad opera sua infra dictas terras meas quoties indigeant de boscis et silvis de Acquhorsk absque impedimento qualicunque. In cujus rei testimonium sigillum meum presenti carte apposui apud Lesley penultimo die mensis Maij. Anno Domini Millesimo trecentesimo nonogesimo primo. Testibus venerabili patre Domino Gylberto Aberdonensi Episcopo. Jacobo Fraser. Domino . de Frendracht. Alexandro Fraser Domino de Phylorth. Johanne de Gordon Domino Ejusdem. Andrea de Lesley (third Baron of Balquhain) consanguineo meo carissimo militibus, et aliis multis.

Original Charter in Balquhain Charter-room.

APPENDIX No. X.

VIII. Sir Andrew de Leslie, Dominus Ejusdem.

Charter by Robert III., confirming a Charter granted by the deceased Norman de Leslie, Knight, to Sir John Ramsay of Culathy.

Robertus omnibus probis hominibus — Sciatis — nos quandam cartam quondam Normani de Lesley militis de mandato nostro — in hac forma — omnibus hanc cartam visuris vel auditurus Normanus de Lesley miles Dominus de Balnabrech salutem in Domino . Noveritis nos post quandam inquisitionem fidedignorum ad hoc juratorum captam apud Glenduky quinto decimo die mensis Julii Anno Domini Millesimo ccc^{mo} nonogesimo quorum nomina sunt hec Andreas de Ramesay de Redy Johannes de Kynnore Willelmus de Berclay Joannes de Cama Alanus de Lochmalony Walterus de Ramesay Maliseus de Kynynmond Johannes de Kyndeloch Willelmus Stirk Willelmus de Ferny Johannes de Ramesay Willelmus de Lochmalony Robertus Lyel Andreas de Cama et Johannes de Arous plenarie intelexisse quod quondam predecessores Domini de Ramesay de Culathy militis infeodati fuerunt de terris de Balmadyside et de Petachop cum pertinenciis hereditarie per quondam Marioriam de Dundemour dominam ejusdem Reddendo sibi et heredibus suis annuatim unum denarium nomine albe firme si petatur ad festum Pentecostes Et nobis et heredibus nostris servicium de dictis terris debitum et consuetum Quam quidem infeodacionem pro nobis et heredibus nostris et successoribus in omnibus suis punctis et articulis modis formis et circumstanciis in omnibus et per omnia ratificamus confirmamus et per presentes approbamus salvo servicio nostro In cujus rei testimonium huic presenti carte sigillum nostrum est appensum apud Balnabrech quintodecimo die mensis Augusti Anno Domini millesimo ccc^{mo} nonogesimo Quam quidem cartam predictam in omnibus punctis suis et articulis condicionibus et modis ac circumstanciis suis quibuscunque &c . in omnibus et per omnia approbamus ratificamus et pro nobis et heredibus nostris ut premissum est imperpetuum confirmamus salvo servicio nostro In cujus rei testimonium presenti carte nostre confirmacionis nostrum precepimus apponi sigillum Testibus venerabilibus in Christo patribus Waltero et Matheo Sancti Andree et Glasguensis ecclesiarum episcopis Roberto de Ffyf et de Meneteth fratre nostro carissimo Archebaldo de Douglas Domino Galwidie consanguineo nostro comitibus Jacobo de Douglas Domino de Dalketh Thoma de Erskine consanguineis nostris militibus et Alexandro de Cokburne de Langtone Custode Magni Sigilli nostri Apud Dunde septimo die Aprilis Anno regni nostri secundo . (A.D. 1392). •

Registrum Magni Sigilli, p. 208, No. 37.

APPENDIX No. XI.

GEORGE LESLIE, SECOND BARON OF THAT ILK.

RESIGNATION in the King's hand, by GEORGE LESLIE, Second Baron of that Ilk, of the lands of Brawkawche, Myddiltone, Knock of Kynblewis, Drummeis, Glaschawe, Mill of Glaschawe, and the Wood of Drumcontane, in the regality of the Garioch, in favour of PATRICK GORDON of Methlic—A.D. 1490-1500.

EXCELLENTISSIMO et inuictissimo principi Jacobo quarto Dei gratia Scotorum Regi illustrissimo vester humilis legius et subditus Georgius Leslie de Eodem . . . In manus vestre serenitatis ego . . . terras nostras de Brawkawche Myddiltone Knok de Kynblewis Drummeis Glaschawe molendinum de Glaschawe et siluam de Drumcontane cum siuis pertinentiis jacentes in regalitate de Gareauche infra vicecomitatum de Aberdene quas de vobis teneo in capite . . . sim-

APPENDIX XI.

plicter resigno . . . pro qua resignatione . . . fienda . . . constituo . . . nobiles et honorabiles viros Walterum Ogiluy de Boyne militem Magistros Willelmum Ogiluy et Alexandrum Ogiluy Andream Wode de Fethercarne . . . meos . . . procuratores . . . in fauorem specialem Patricii Gordon de Methtlik . . . In cujus rei testimonium presentibus sigillum meum est appensum apud . . .

Antiquities of the Shires of Aberdeen and Banff, vol. iii. p. 472, Spalding Club. From Notary's protocol, entitled, "Register of Sasines for the Burgh of Aberdeen," vol. i. MS. in archivis ejusdem.

Appendix XII.

APPENDIX No. XII.

GEORGE LESLIE, SECOND BARON OF THAT ILK.

CHARTER of half of the lands of Edingarioch, and half of the lands of Chapeltown, granted by King JAMES IV. to GEORGE LESLIE, Second Baron of that Ilk, and VIOLET MIDDLETON his Spouse—24th November 1497.

1497.

JACOBUS Dei gracia Rex Scotorum . . . Sciatis nos tanquam tutorem et gubernatorem carissimi fratris nostri Johannis Comitis de Mar et Garriache dedissi . . . dilectis nostris Georgio Leslie de Eodem et Violete Myddiltoun, ejus sponse et ipsorum alteri diucius viuenti in conjuncta infeodacione dimidietatem terrarum de Edingarrach et dimidietatem terrarum de le Chapeltoun cum suis pertinenciis jacentes in regalitate de Garriache infra vicecomitatum nostrum de Aberdene Quequidem terre cum pertinenciis fuerunt dicti Georgii hereditarie et quas idem Georgius non vi aut metu ductus . . . in manus nostras apud Linlytgow tanquam in manibus tutoris prefati carissimi fratris nostri Johannis Comitis de Mar domini superioris earundem per fustem et baculum . . . simpliciter resignauit . . . Tenendas . . . de prefato carissimo fratre nostro Johanne Comite de Mar et suis successoribus in feodo et hereditate in perpetuum . . .

THE FAMILY OF LESLIE.

Faciendo inde annuatim prefato Comiti de Mar et suis successoribus jura et seruicia de dictis terris cum pertinenciis ante dictam resignacionem debita et consueta. In cuius rei testimonium presenti carte nostre resignacionis magnum sigillum nostrum apponi precipimus. Testibus reuerendo in Christo Patre Willelmo Episcopo Aberdonensi nostri secreti sigilli custode dilectis consanguineis Archibaldo Comite de Ergyle Domino Campbell et Lorne magistro hospicii nostri . . . Apud Linlytgow vicesimo quarto die mensis Nouembris anno Domini millesimo quadringentesimo nonagesimo septimo et regni nostri decimo.

APPENDIX XII.

1497.

Collections on Shires of Aberdeen and Banff, p. 551 ; from the Earl of Haddington's Collection of Charters, vol. i. p. 273, MS.

APPENDIX No. XIII.

GEORGE LESLIE, SECOND OF THAT ILK.

CONFIRMATION by King JAMES IV. to GEORGE LESLIE, Second of that Ilk, and MARGARET FRASER his Wife, of Eight Mercates of the lands of Chapeltoune, in the Lordship of the Garioch—A.D. 1505.

Appendix XIII.

1505.

APUD Abirdene . xxvi (Octobris) . j^m v v . . Rex confirmavit Georgio Leslie de eodem et Margrete Frasere ejus sponse et eorum alteri diucius viventi in conjuncta infeodatione et post eorum decessum legitimis et propinquioribus heredibus dicti Georgii quibuscunque octo mercatas terrarum de Chapeltoune in dominio de Garviauche infra vicecomitatum de Abirdene quas dictus Georgius personaliter resignavit.

Antiquities of Shires of Aberdeen and Banff, vol. iii. p. 391, Spalding Club. From the *Abbrevatio Registri Magni Sigilli*, lib. xiv. No. 154, MS. General Register House, Edinburgh.

APPENDIX No. XIV.
ALEXANDER LESLIE, FOURTH OF THAT ILK.

CHARTER by ALEXANDER LESLIE, and CHRISTIAN LESLIE his Wife, fiars of the Barony of Leslie, with consent of JONET LESLIE, liferenter of the same, to the Chaplains of the Choir of the Collegiate Church of Aberdeen, of an annual rent of Forty Shillings from the lands of the Manor of Leslie—A.D. 1527.

OMNIBUS hanc cartam visuris . . . Alexander Lesley et Cristina Lesley eius sponsa feodatarii . . . terrarum baronie de Lesley salutem . . . Noueritis nos cum . . . consensu . . . nobilis domicelle Jonete Lesley francmentarii et vsufructuarii terrarum dicte baronie pro toto tempore vite ejusdem . . . dedisse . . . ac titulo pure venditionis alienasse . . . Magistris Johanni Awaill Alexandro Wrycht Duncano Robertsone et Dauid Barnys ceterisque Capellanis chori ecclesie collegiate Abirdonensis et eorundem successoribus . . . vnum annuum redditum quadraginta solidorum . . . monete . . . Scocie annuatim de terris nostris maneriei de Lesley et pertinentiis eiusdem jacentibus infra baroniam de Lesley et vicecomitatum de Abirdene . . . Tenendum . . . hujusmodi annuum redditum . . . de nobis heredibus nostris dictarumque terrarum possessoribus in alba firma . . . Ac in speciale warrantum damus . . . terras baronie nostre de Petnamwin jacentes infra vicecomitatum de Kyncardyn et baroniam de Balmain . . . In cuius rei testimonium sigilla nostra propria presentibus sunt appensa unacum sigillo dicte Jonete in signum sui consensus . . . Apud Abirdene none die mensis Augusti anno Domini millesimo quingentesimo vigesimo septimo coram his testibus Magistris Waltero Stewart Thoma Pyot et Thoma Lesley unacum subscriptione manuali Alexandri Lesley.

ALEX^R. LESLIE of that Ilk, with my hand.

Antiquities of Shires of Aberdeen and Banff, vol. iii. p. 392, Spalding Club. From the original in the possession of the late Patrick Rose, Esq., Sheriff-Clerk of Banffshire.

APPENDIX No. XV.

ALEXANDER LESLIE, FOURTH OF THAT ILK.

INSTRUMENT upon the presentation by ALEXANDER LESLIE, fourth of that Ilk, for himself, and in the name of JOHN LESLIE his son and heir, to MARGARET LESLIE, Daughter of the deceased ALEXANDER LESLIE, third of that Ilk, of JOHN LESLIE, or Master THOMAS MORTYMAR, as a fit Husband for her—A.D. 1544.

VIGESIMO primo Januarii Anno Domini etc xliij° Eodem die Alexander Leslie, de Eodem pro se et procuratorio nomine Johannis Leslie sui filii primogeniti et heredis apparentis ipso presente et consentiente accessit ad personalem presentiam honorabilis damicelle Margarete Leslie filie quondam Alexandri Leslie de Eodem qui obtulit eedem Margarete comparem ad contrahendum matrimonium videlicet Johannem Leslie eius fratrem germanum vel Magistrum Thomam Mortymar ad placitum dicte Margarete quem habere voluerit et si obstat impedimentum consanguinitatis vel affinitatis ad obtinendum dispensationem summi pontificis fideliter promisit quod si refutauerit et aliter aut cum aliquo contraxerit matrimonium de remedio juris solempniter protestatus est Super quibus idem Alexander pro se et procuratorio nomine dicti sui filii a me notario petiit instrumentum Acta erant hec in aula de Leslie hora quasi pomeridiana quarta presentibus Domino Willelmo Cristesone Magistro Thoma Mortimar Thoma Red Alexandro Pattone et me notario publico.

Antiquities of Shires of Aberdeen and Banff, voL iii. p. 392, Spalding Club. From the General Register House, Edinburgh.

APPENDIX No. XVI.

JOHN LESLIE, FIFTH OF THAT ILK.

LEASE for nineteen years by JOHN, Abbot of Lindores, and the Monks of the same, to JOHN LESLIE, fifth of that Ilk, and ELIZABETH DEMPSTER his Wife, of the Teind-Sheaves of the Mains of Leslie, Auld Leslie, and Curtastoun—A.D. 1546.

UNIVERSIS . . . nos Johannem . . . abbatem monasterii de Lundoris et ejusdem loci conventus . . . salutem . . . Noueritis nos . . . vnanimi consensu . . . pro summa triginta librarum monete Scocie . . . per subscriptum honorabilem virum Johannem Leslie de Eodem nobis gratanter persoluta . . . ad firmam dimisisse . . . prefato Johanni Lesly de Eodem Elizabeth Dempster eius sponse et eorum alteri diutius viuenti quibus deficientibus eorum vnico assignato et subtenentibus pluribus aut vni non maioris potentie seipsis . . . decimas nostras garbales de Manys de Leslie Auld Leslie et Curtastoun cum . . . pertinentiis jacentibus infra parochiam ecclesie nostre de Leslie et vicecomitatum de Abirden pro omnibus terminis nouemdecim annorum . . . Soluendo inde annuatim . . . summam quadraginta duarum marcarum monete Scocie videlicet pro decimis garbalibus de lie Manys de Leslie nouem marcas et pro decimis garbalibus de Auld Leslie tredecim marcas et pro decimis garbalibus de Curtaston viginti marcas . . . ad festum Sancti Laurentii Marthiris aut scilicet ad Festum Sancti Bartholmei annuatim . . . In cuius rei testimonium sigillum commune capituli nostri presenti nostre assedationi est appensum ac nostris subscriptionibus manualibus subscripte apud dictum monasterium de Lundoris die decimo mensis Octobris anno Domini millesimo quingentesimo quadragesimo sexto coram hiis testibus venerabilibus et honorabilibus viris Magistris Jacobo Rolland priore de Balquhidder Roberto Lausoun Johanne Rolland Johanne Philp vicario de Logiedurno

Henrico Philip Michaele Inch Jacobo Smyth Andrea Paigh et Johanne Bennat cum diversis aliis.

    Johannes Abbot of Lundoris.   Alex^r. Patonson.
    Johannes Brownhill supprior   Robertus Jameson.
       ejusdem.   Robertus Wilyemson.
    Johannes Blair.   Robertus Wostuatter.
    Ricardus Barcar.   Jacobus Carstairs.
    Patricius Steill.   Johannes Skynnir.
    Willelmus Messon.   Willelmus Walhand.
    Alex^r. Wrycht.   Gilbertus Mischell.
    Alex^r. Ricardsoun.   Andreas Vod.
    Daniel Orem.   Johannes Smyth.
    Andreas Lesly.

Antiquities of the Shires of Aberdeen and Banff, vol. iii. p. 393, Spalding Club. From the original in the possession of the late Patrick Rose, Esq., Sheriff-Clerk of Banffshire.

APPENDIX No. XVII.

JOHN LESLIE, FIFTH OF THAT ILK.

FEU-CHARTER by SIR THOMAS RAITH, Vicar of the parish church of Leslie, with consent of JOHN, Abbot of Lindores, and the Monks of the same, to JOHN LESLIE, fifth of that Ilk, of the Kirklands and Glebe of the Vicarage of Leslie—A.D. 1561.

OMNIBUS hanc cartam visuris . . . Dominus Thomas Raith vicarius ecclesie parochialis de Leslie salutem . . . (Noveritis me) . . . cum consensu . . . Johannis abbatis monasterii de Lundoris et conuentus eiusdem . . . exigentibus . . . nonnullis gratitudinibus et benemeritis honorabilis viri Johannis Leslie de eodem ac pro certa summa pecunie . . . ad feudifirmam . . . hereditarie dimisisse . . . prefato Johanni suis heredibus et assignatis . . . terras meas ecclesiasticas cum gleba prefate mee vicarie de Leslie cum

APPENDIX XVII.

suis pertinentiis jacentes infra diocesim Aberdonensem et vicecomitatum ejusdem Tenendas ... de me et successoribus meis vicariis dicte ecclesie in feudifirma ... imperpetuum ... Reddendo inde annuatim ... michi et successoribus meis summam quatuor marcarum ... monete ... Scotie tanquam firmam ... solitam necnon duos solidos ... in augmentationem rentalis ... Insuper dilectis meis Roberto Leslie in Auchmair Nicholao Murray ... balliuis meis ... vobis precipio ... quatenus ... sasinam ... prefatarum terrarum prefatis Johanni vel suo certo attornato latori presentium ... tradatis ... reseruata michi et successoribus meis manerea seu mansione dicte vicarie cum seminatione duarum bollarum ordei ex orientali parte crofte de Gostach quequidem crofta una pars dictarum terrarum ecclesiasticarum est In cujus rei testimonium huic presenti infeodationi mee manu mea subscripte sigillum meum proprium est appensum una cum sigillo communi capituli dicti monasterii et subscriptionibus manualibus dictorum Abbatis et Conuentus in signum eorum consensus ... ad premissa ... apud Edinburght et Lundoris respectiue

1561.

primo die mensis Maii anno Domini millesimo quingentesimo sexagesimo primo coram his testibus Magistro Joanne Leslie rectore de Wne Magistro Roberto Lummisdane de Clovay et Archibaldo Dempster in Coschenay cum diuersis aliis.

Thomas Raith vicar of Leslie wyth my hand.	Willelmus Symson.
	Andreas Froster.
Johannes, Abbot of Lundoris.	Thomas Woid.
Jacobus Carstaris.	Johannes Smyth.
Alexander Patonsone.	Gilbertus Mischell.
Robertus Wilyemson.	Johannes Wobster.

Antiquities of Shires of Aberdeen and Banff, vol. iii. p. 390, Spalding Club. From original in the possession of the late Patrick Rose, Esq., Sheriff-Clerk of Banffshire.

APPENDIX No. XVIII.

JOHN LESLIE, FIFTH OF THAT ILK.

LEASE for twice nineteen years of the Teinds of the Mains of Leslie, and the lands of Edingarrah, by JOHN LESLIE, Vicar of Pramoth, with consent of the President and Chapter of Aberdeen, to JOHN LESLIE fifth of that Ilk—A.D. 1579.

BE it kende till all men . . . me Jhone Leslie vicar perpetuall of Pramoth . . . within the regalite of Garyeaucht diosie and shirefdome of Aberdene . . . with consent of the Precedent and Chaptur of Abirdene . . . to have sett . . . to ane honorabill man Jhone Leslie of that Ilk and to his airs and assignais . . . the vicarage of the Manes of Leslie and of haill landis of Edingarrah sa far as lyis within the paroche of Pramay . . . that is to say teind hay teind nolt teind cheis teind lint teind   and all otheris emolumentis pertening or may pertene to the wicarage of the saidis landis with thair pertinentis . . . for the haill space of thre yeris . . . following the entres thairto quhilk . . . sal be at the Feist of the Inuentione of the Cross callit the Ruid day the yere of God ane thousand fywe hundretht sewinte and aucht yeris and fra thre yeris to thre yeris indvringe the space of nyntene yeris . . . and frae thre yeris to thre yeris indvring the space of wthir nyntene yeris . . . following the first nyntene yeris . . . Payand thairfor yerlie . . . to me and my successoris . . . the soume of fourte schillingis Scottis monie at the Feist of Pashe allanarlie . . . In witnes of the quhilkis to this my assedatione subscriuit with my hand togyddir with the subscriptionis of the said Presedent and Chanonis my seall is appensit to the same at Abirdeyne the twenty sewint of Januare the yere of God ane thousand fywe hundretht sewinte and aucht yeris befoir thir witnes Andrew Annand masar burges of Doundie Valter Leslie in Auld Leslie Malcolme Layng Alexander Clerk in Kyntor and Maister Robert Roust notair public Maisteris Robert Lumisden of Clowat Williame Dauidsone and Gilbert Ross notair publict.

      Johnne Leslye vicar of Premnaucht with my hand.
      Aberdonensis Episcopus.
      Willelmus Setone Cancellarius Aberdonensis.
      Jacobus Erskine Archidiaconus Aberdonensis.
      Mr. Robert Merser of Banquhory Devynik.
      John Collison subchantur of Abd.
      Mr. Thomas Burnett personn of Methlik.

Antiquities of Shires of Aberdeen and Banff, vol. iii. p. 399, Spalding Club. From the original in possession of the late Patrick Rose, Esq., Sheriff-Clerk of Banffshire.

APPENDIX No. XIX.

THE EARLDOM OF ROSS.

THE territorial dignity of the earldom of Ross existed at a very early period. There was a succession of earls of Ross from the period that the parliament was held at Forfar or Angus by King Malcolm III. about 1061.

The chief residence of the Earls of Ross was the castle of Dingwall, which stood at the east end of the town of Dingwall, close to the shore, on the firth of Cromarty. The deep stormy river Peffery wound round two sides of the castle, and a plain of some extent surrounded the other two sides. The castle was strongly fortified, and the fosse and glace may still be traced.

The Earls of Ross possessed a great part of the lands in the district of Ross, and many rich baronies in various counties in Scotland. Even now many proprietors hold their lands by charters granted by the Earls of Ross, and dated from "our castle of Dingwall."

I. MALCOLM, the first Earl of Ross of whom we have any account, was possessor of the earldom in the reign of Mal-

THE FAMILY OF LESLIE.

colm IV., who directed a precept to Malcolm, Earl of Ross, to protect and defend the monks of Dunfermline in their lawful privileges and possessions, witnessed by Arnold, Bishop of St. Andrews, who died in 1162.* He was succeeded by

II. FERQUHARD, Earl of Ross, who accompanied Alexander II. to London about 1227. He there challenged a renowned French champion to single combat, and made a vow to found a monastery in his own earldom if he conquered his opponent. Having vanquished and slain his antagonist, the earl set about to accomplish his vow. He travelled home, and brought with him from the priory of Candida Casa in Galloway two canons who founded an abbey at Fearn, in the earldom of Ross. The abbey was situated in the parish of Eddertown, on the firth of Dornoch in Ross-shire. The first abbot was Malcolm of Galloway, appointed in 1230; the second was Malcolm of Nigg, who succeeded about 1246. Hector Boece asserts that for the gallant deed of overcoming the Frenchman the king conferred the earldom of Ross on Ferquhard Ross, who was only a private gentleman. But there are proofs that there were Earls of Ross long previous to this period. Ferquhard, Earl of Ross, is a witness to the treaty between Alexander II. of Scotland and Henry III. of England, dated at York, September 1237, and also to many charters granted during the reign of Alexander II. Dominus Fercardus, Comes de Ross, is a witness to a composition between Andrew, Bishop of Moray, and William Cumyn, Earl of Mynynteth, concerning the lands of Kynkardyn, in 1234;† to a composition between the Chapter of Moray and Alexander de Stryvelene, concerning the half-darach of land at Devath, in 1234;‡ to a composition between Andrew, Bishop of Moray, and Walter de Moravia de Duffus, concerning the lands of Ewin, VII. Idus Augusti,

APPENDIX XIX.

1662.

1227.

1230.
1246.

1237.

1234.

---

* *Chartulary of Dunfermline*, No. 186 D.
† *Registrum Moraviense*, p. 99, No. 85.
‡ *Ibid.* p. 99, No. 86.

APPENDIX XIX.

1235.* He granted a charter of two dovates of the lands of Clon in Ross, to Walter de Moravia, son of Hugh de Moravia, to be held in feu and heritage for the yearly payment of a pound of pepper.† He was succeeded by his son

III. WILLIAM, third Earl of Ross. William, son and heir of Ferquhard, Earl of Ross, is one of the witnesses to the charter granted by Earl Ferquhard to Walter de Moravia. He is also one of the witnesses to an agreement between Andrew, Bishop of Moray, and Gilbert, son of the Earl of Strathen, dated Anno gratie 1232, pridie Idus Septembris.‡ He confirmed all his father's grants and donations to the abbey of Fearn in 1258, and made donations to the religious in Moray by deeds witnessed by Robert, Bishop of Ross, who died in 1270.§ He was Justiciary of Scotland north of the Forth, as appears by a precept from him to David Wemys, Sheriff of Fife, 7th October, Anno Regni Alexandri II. vicesimo quinto, A.D. 1239, commanding David Wemys to pay the eighth part of the amercements of Fife imposed in the Justice Aire of Cupar, to the Abbot of Dunfermline, according to his rights.|| In the time of Archibald, Bishop of Moray, who was consecrated in 1253, and died 5th December 1298, it seems that William, Earl of Ross, had done some injury to the church of Pettie, and to the prebendary of Brachlie, for the reparation of which he gave the lands of Catboll in Ross, and other lands, to the Bishop and canons of Moray. ¶ William, Earl of Ross, was one of the Scottish nobles who entered into an agreement with Llewellyn, Prince of Wales, that the Scotch and Welsh should not make peace with England without the mutual consent of both—8th March 1258. He was also one of the nobles who signed the obligation which Alexander III. obtained from his chief nobility to receive as Queen of Scotland his granddaughter Margaret, the

1232.

1258.

1270.

1239.

1253.
1298.

1258.

---

* *Registrum Moraviense*, p. 101, No. 87. † *Ibid.* p. 333, No. 259.
‡ *Ibid.* p. 89, No. 80. § *Chartulary of Moray*, pp. 312-317.
|| *Chartulary of Dunfermline.*
¶ Shaw's *History of Moray*, p. 170.

THE FAMILY OF LESLIE.   169

Maiden of Norway, and the issue of her body—dated at Scone, 5th February 1288, and signed by

    Alexander de Cumyn, Comes de Buchan, Constabularius.
    Malesius, Comes de Strathern.
    Johannes de Baleolo.
    Alexander de Baleolo.
    Robertus de Bruce, Comes de Carrick.
    Robertus de Bruce, Pater.
    Willelmus, Comes de Ross.
    Gilbert, Comes de Angus.
    Willelmus, Comes de Sutherland.
    Magnus, Comes de Cathenea.
    Jacobus, Senescalus Scocie.
    Nicholâs de Haya;
    and others.

William, third Earl of Ross, died about 1289, and was succeeded by his son

IV. WILLIAM, fourth earl. The Earls of Ross, Athole, Moray, and others, were witnesses to the confirmation by King Robert I. of Scotland, and Haquin, King of Norway, at Inverness, 28th October 1312, of a treaty between Alexander III. of Scotland and Magnus IV. of Norway, 6th July 1266, whereby Magnus renounced for ever the Isles of Sodor and Man, and all the Western Isles, for an annual rent of one hundred merks sterling, and the sum of four thousand merks to be paid by instalments; reserving, however, to himself the Isles of Orkney and Shetland. William, Earl of Ross, is also one of the witnesses to a charter whereby Robert I. granted the lands of Taruays, or Tarves, in Aberdeenshire, to the Abbey of Arbroath, 26th February 1313.* He got a charter from Robert I. of the lands of Dingwall, with the castle, burgh, and liberties of the same, and other lands, in 1321;† also another charter, dated 5th August 1322, witnessed by Donald, Abbot of

---

    * *Registrum vetus Cenobii de Aberbrothoc.*
   † Robertson's *Index of Missing Charters*, No. 15.

APPENDIX XIX.	New Fearn. He appeared in the convention of Brigham, 12th March 1289, when the marriage of Queen Margaret with Prince Edward of England was proposed. He was one of the nominees on the part of Baliol in his competition
1292.	for the crown of Scotland with Robert Bruce, 1292. He swore fealty to Edward I. at Berwick, 3d August 1292, and was present when John Baliol did homage to the English king, 20th November 1292. He was directed to attend Edward at London, 1st September 1294, to go over
1294.	the seas with the king, by letters dated 29th June 1294. He was in the Scottish army at the battle of Dunbar, 28th
1296.	April 1296, and, after the defeat of the Scots, he took refuge in the castle of Dunbar, which was surrendered a day or two afterwards, and he was carried prisoner to
1308.	London. He adhered to Edward II., who, 20th May 1308, addressed a letter to him and his son Hugh, thanking them for past services and requiring their aid. Afterwards he joined the party of Robert Bruce, and was one of the guarantees of a treaty between him and Edward II., 1st
1323.	June 1323. He was one of the nobles who signed the
1320.	letter addressed to Pope John XXII. in 1320, asserting the independence of Scotland.

William, fourth Earl of Ross, had three children—

    I. HUGH, who succeeded him.
    II. JOHN, who married Margaret Cumyn, second daughter of Alexander, fourth Earl of Buchan, and got with her as tocher half of the Earl of Buchan's lands in Scotland ;

1315.	and Robert I., in 1315, confirmed a charter granting to them these lands.*

    III. LADY ISABELLA, married to Edward Bruce, Earl of Carrick, for which marriage a papal dispensation was

1317.	obtained, 1st June 1317.
1328.	William, fourth Earl of Ross, died before 3d July 1328, and was succeeded by his eldest son,

V. HUGH, fifth Earl, who had charters from King Robert I. to himself and his wife, Maud, the king's sister, of the

---

* Robertson's *Index*, Nos. 41, 42.

THE FAMILY OF LESLIE.

lands of Nairn, with the town, and of the town of Crumbachie, or Cromarty, with an annual rent. He had also charters of the thanage of Glendouachy in Banffshire: of the lands of Sky, of Trouterness in Sky, of Tarnedelle and Innerafren, of Straglass and Strathconan; of Kinfauns in Perthshire, with the fishings; and to him and his spouse, of the barony of Inverlunan. He had a controversy with Andrew de Moravia concerning the lands of Dromcudyn, Munlochy, and others, 3d July 1328. King Edward III. ratified a treaty with King Robert I. at Northampton, 4th May 1328, for a marriage between David, son and heir of Robert I., and Johanna, sister of Edward III., both then under age, and Hugh, Earl of Ross, and Robert de Lawdor, Justiciary of Lothian, swore that all the articles of the treaty would be observed. Hugh, Earl of Ross, resigned into the king's hands the patronage of the church of Philorth in Buchan, 29th March 1330.

He married first Jean, daughter of Walter, High Steward of Scotland, but does not seem to have had any issue by her; he married, secondly, Maud, sister of King Robert Bruce, and had issue—

I. WILLIAM, who succeeded him.
II. HUGH ROSS of Rarichies, of whom there are several notices in Robertson's *Index*. A safe-conduct was granted, 3d September 1351, to Hugh Ross, brother and presumptive heir of the Earl of Ross, as one of the hostages for David II. when the king was allowed to visit his dominions in that year. Hugh de Ross, Lord of Philorth, son of the deceased Hugh, Earl of Ross, granted a charter to Adam Urquhart, Sheriff of Cromarty, of the lands of Fohesterdy in Buchan, 1st August 1365. He also granted a charter to Alexander de Santo Claro of the lands of Estirtyre in Aberdeenshire. David II. granted a charter of ten pounds and four chalders of wheat due to the king out of the lands of Doun in Banffshire, to Hugo de Ross, and Margaret de Barclay his spouse, 26th February 1369. Another charter of the same was granted to Hugh de Roos de Kynfaunys,

APPENDIX XIX.

1328.

1330.

1351.

1365.

1369.

and Margaret his spouse, by Robert II., 1st June 1373. Hugh de Ross seems to have died soon after this, as Robert II., 10th August 1374, granted a charter ratifying a grant made by the late William, Earl of Ross, "our brother," to the late Hugh de Ross, his brother, of the lands of Balnagoune, Achanyll, and Corty, and an annual rent of four pounds from Tarbard in the earldom of Ross, to be held by William de Ross, son and heir of the said late Hugh, and his heirs. From this Hugh de Ross descended Munro Ross of Pitcalnie, who, in February 1778, presented a petition to the king, showing that the title and dignity of Earl of Ross was very ancient, and was limited to and held in the male line till the death of William, Earl of Ross, in 1370 ; that the said William, Earl of Ross, dying without male issue, left two daughters—Lady Eufamia, who married Sir Walter Leslie, and Lady Johanna, who married Sir Alexander Fraser ; that the said Earl of Ross left a brother, Hugh Ross of Rarichies, who, as heir-male, was entitled to take the title and dignity of Earl of Ross, but being opposed and oppressed by the power and influence of the husbands of his nieces, and also by the Duke of Albany, Regent of Scotland, he was obliged to submit to their usurpation of his rights ; that the petitioner was the male descendant of the foresaid Hugh Ross of Rarichies, brother of the last Earl of Ross and, as such was entitled to the foresaid title and dignity. Therefore he humbly prayed the king that the title and dignity of Ross, Earl of Ross, might be declared of right to belong to him and his heirs-male. By the king's command the petition was presented to the House of Lords, 9th February 1778, but no determination appears to have been come to thereon.

III. LADY LILIAS, married to William Urchard of Cromarty, who was hereditary sheriff of that county in the reign of Robert Bruce, 1306-1329. Their son, Adam Urchard, got from William, sixth Earl of Ross, a charter of the lands of Inchrory in Ross, dated 30th September 1338 ;

THE FAMILY OF LESLIE.

and also charters of the davach lands of Bray, dated at Dingwall, 6th January 1349.

IV. LADY EUFAMIA, married, first, to John Randolph, Earl of Moray, who was killed at the battle of Durham, in 1346; secondly, to Robert, Earl of Strathern, afterwards King Robert II., for which marriage a papal dispensation was obtained 2d May 1355.

V. LADY JANET, married, first, to Monymusk of Monymusk; and secondly, to Sir Alexander Moray of Abercairney.

Hugh, Earl of Ross, and Kenneth, Earl of Sutherland, commanded the advanced guard of the Scottish army at the battle of Halidon Hill, 22d July 1333, when the Earl of Ross was slain. He was succeeded by his eldest son,

VI. WILLIAM, sixth Earl of Ross, who granted a charter to his nephew, Adam Urchard, the son of his sister Lilias, of the lands of Inchrory in Ross, 30th September 1338, and of the davach lands of Bray, 6th January 1349. He also granted a charter to Reginald, son of Roderick of the Isles, of ten davits of the lands of Kennetale, dated at the castle of Urchard, 4th July 1342, and confirmed by David II. in the following year. He granted a charter to Robert Munro, eighth Baron of Foulis, of the lands of Pittende and others, for payment of a pair of white gloves and three pennies Scots. A treaty was signed at Berwick, 3d October 1357, for liberating David II., who had been taken prisoner at Durham in 1346. His ransom was 100,000 merks, to be paid by instalments of 10,000 merks annually for ten years, and twenty hostages were to be given for the payment, three of the following six nobleman to be always of the number of hostages—viz. John, eldest son and heir of Robert, Steward of Scotland; the Earls of Ross, Mar, and Sutherland; Lord Douglas, and Thomas de Moray. William, Earl of Ross, is a witness to a charter granted by David II. in August 1359, to the chapel of the Virgin at Inverness, of a portion of the lands of Cras, confirmed in full parliament at Scone, 26th October 1359.* He granted to the

---

* *Registrum Moraviense*, p. 302, No. 234.

chapel of the Virgin at Inverness four merks of annual rent out of the lands of Culdochy, by a charter dated at Spynie, Thursday after the feast of St. Peter ad vincula, 1361.* As superior of the lands of Brythmond and Kynstary, he confirmed a charter of an annual rent of one hundred shillings sterling out of the said lands granted by Robert de Laweder for the foundation of a chapel in the cathedral of Moray, dated at Dunfermline, 1st May 1362.† He granted to the cathedral of Moray an annual rent of four merks out of the lands of Culdochy, 20th February 1365.‡ He confirmed a charter, 21st December 1366, granted by his brother, Hugh de Ross, Dominus de Philorth, son of Hugh, Earl of Ross, to Adam Urchard, Sheriff of Cromarty, of the lands of Fochesterday, or Fishery in Buchan, which charter was confirmed by David II. at Montrose, 8th December 1368. David II. regranted to William, Earl of Ross, the forest of Plater, and the lands of Fythinewyest, and the patronage of the church, on the earl's resignation, 6th May 1369.§ William, Earl of Ross, Lord of Sky, granted a charter to his brother, Hugh Ross, of Rarichies, of the lands of Kilmachalmark and Carbisdile, reserving the salmon-fishing of the Kyle of Ockil, dated at Dingwall, 4th February 1370. David II. confirmed a charter to William, Earl of Ross, of all the earldom of Ross, and Lordship of Sky, and failing him and the heirs-male of his body, to Sir Walter Leslie, knight, and Eufamia Ross his wife, dated at Perth, 23d October 1370. David II. confirmed a grant made by William, Earl of Ross, to Alexander de Sancto Claro, of the lands of Bray in Inverness, dated at Dundee, 1st November 1370.|| He also confirmed a charter granted by William, Earl of Ross, to Hugh de Ross, of the lands of Philorth and Easter Tyre in Aberdeenshire. John de Haya, Dominus de Tulybotheyle, with the consent

---

* *Registrum Moraviense*, p. 306, No. 237.
† *Ibid.* p. 309, No. 239.   ‡ *Ibid.* p. 317, No. 243.
§ *Registrum Magni Sigilli Regum Scotorum*, p. 65, No. 215.
|| *Registrum Magni Sigilli*, p. 76, No. 274.

THE FAMILY OF LESLIE.

formerly obtained of the late William, Earl of Ross, his superior, granted several lands to found a chapel of the blessed Virgin at Kincragy, by a charter, dated at Rate, 3d May 1374.*

William, Earl of Ross, was Justiciary of Scotland north of the Forth in 1342. When David II. resolved to invade England, and appointed an army to assemble at Perth in 1346, for that purpose, William, Earl of Ross, and Reginald of the Isles, appeared at the rendezvous, where the Earl of Ross, having a difference with Reginald, assassinated him at the monastery of Elcho, and abandoned the king's host, and led his followers back to their mountains. Robert Munro, Baron of Foulis, was killed in a scuffle, in defence of William, Earl of Ross, in 1369.

William, Earl of Ross, married, first, Isabel, daughter of Malesius, Earl of Strathern, Caithness, and Orkney, who, according to Sir Robert Gordon, in 1344 gave the earldom of Caithness to William, Earl of Ross, in marriage with his daughter Isabel, by a charter confirmed by David II. in 1362. The issue of this marriage was—

I. WILLIAM. Among the hostages proposed for the release of David II., 13th July 1354, was the son and heir of the Earl of Ross, when he was of an age to travel, or the brother of the said Earl. In August 1357, in naming hostages for the king, it was stated that William, filz et heir le Counte de Rosse est malades, et le roi David, &c., sont compris qu'il serra livere s'il soit en vie devant Nowel, et s'il soit mort, que le prochain heir au dit Counte vendra en son lieu. William died without issue before his father.

II. LADY EUFAMIA, who married Sir Walter Leslie, and, in consequence of the charter of 23d October 1370, succeeded her father as seventh Countess of Ross.

III. LADY JOHANNA, married to Sir Alexander Fraser of Philorth.

---

* *Registrum Moraviense*, p. 320, No. 245.

APPENDIX XIX.

1371-2.

William, Earl of Ross, is said to have married, secondly, a daughter of Sir David Graham of Montrose, by whom he had a daughter, Margaret, married to Sir Walter Hamilton of Innerwick. He died 1371-2, and was succeeded by his eldest daughter, Eufamia, seventh Countess of Ross.

Appendix XX.

APPENDIX No. XX.

WALTER LESLIE, EARL OF ROSS.

CHARTER by WALTER LESLIE, DOMINUS DE ROSS, to EUFEMIA DE SANCTO CLARO, of the lands of Tiry in Buchan, and of Bra, Drum, and Bron, in the shire of Inverness—A.D. 1367.

1367.

OMNIBUS hoc scriptum visuris vel audituris Walterus de Lesly dominus de Ross / salutem in Domino sempiternam / Sciatis nos dedisse . . . dilecte et fideli nostre Evfemie de Sancto Claro omnes et singulas terras de Bra cum pertinentiis iacentes infra vicecomitatum de Inuerness / et de Tiry infra vicecomitatum de Aberdene / dimidietatem de Drum et tertiam partem de Bron cum pertinentiis infra vicecomitatum de Inuerness / Quequidem terre de Bra et Tiry fuerunt Alexandri de Sancto Claro hereditarie / et que medietas de Drum et terre de Bron fuerunt Elene de Sancto Claro / quasque Alexander et dicta Elena . . . mera et spontanea voluntate in manus nostras per fustum et baculum reddiderunt . . . Tenendas et habendas dicte Eufemie pro se et heredibus suis de nobis et heredibus nostris / dando nobis et heredibus nostris annuatim duos denarios nomine albe firme ad Festum Sancti Johannis Baptiste tantum si petatur / In cuius rei testimonium presenti carte nostre sigillum nostrum precepimus apponi / Testibus Hugone de Fraser / Johanne de le Hay / et Roberto de Innes / cum multis aliis / Anno Domini m°ccc° sexagesimo septimo.

1367.

Antiquities of Shires of Aberdeen and Banff, vol. ii. p. 383. From the original in the Innes Charter-chest at Floors.

APPENDIX No. XXI.

WALTER LESLIE, EARL OF ROSS.

CHARTER by King DAVID II. to Sir WALTER DE LESLIE, and EUFAMIA his spouse, of the lands of the Thanage of Aberchirder and the lands of Blaresnache—A.D. 1369.

DAVID Dei gracia / Rex Scottorum / omnibus probis hominibus tocius terre sue salutem / Sciatis nos dedisse . . . dilecto consanguineo nostro Waltero de Lesley pro fideli seruicio suo nobis impenso et impendendo / omnes et singulas terras nostras thanagii de Abirkyrdore / ac terram nostram de Blaresenache / cum pertinenciis infra vicecomitatum de Banffe / Tendendas et habendas eidem Waltero et Eufamie sponse sue dilecte consanguinee nostre / ac heredibus inter ipsos legitime procreatis seu procreandis / de nobis et heredibus nostris in feodo et hereditate / in vnam integram et liberam baroniam per omnes rectas metas et diuisas suas in boscis et planis . . . necnon cum omnibus aliis et singulis libertatibus commoditatibus . . . libere et quiete . . . Faciendo nobis et heredibus nostris dictus Walterus et Eufamia sponsa sua ac heredes sui predicti / seruicium vnius militis pro dictis terris ac tres sectas curie ad tria placita nostra capitalia vicecomitatus de Banffe / In cuius rei . . . Testibus . . . apud Perthe penultimo die Februarii / anno regni nostri Quadragesimo (A.D. 1369).

Registrum Magni Sigilli Regum Scotorum, p. 71. No. 243.

APPENDIX No. XXII.

WALTER LESLIE, EARL OF ROSS.

CHARTER by King DAVID II. to Sir WALTER DE LESLIE, Knight, of the Thanages of Aberchirder and Kincardine; with a provision that, if the heirs of the old Thanes should recover possession, Sir Walter should have the accustomed Service and Rent paid by them in time past to the Crown—A.D. 1369.

DAVID Dei gracia / Rex Scotorum / omnibus ... Licet alias infeodauerimus dilectum consanguineum nostrum / Walterum de Lesley militem / hereditarie / de thanagio de Abirkiirdore cum pertinenciis infra vicecomitatum de Banff / et de thanagiis de Kyncardyn / tamen / quia forte heredes thanorum qui dicta thanagia antiquitus ad feodam firmam tenuerunt recuperare poterunt infuturum ipsa thanagia tenenda prout eorum predecessores ipsa tenuerunt / concessimus dicto consanguineo nostro quod / si ipsi heredes vel eorum aliquis dicta thanagia vel aliquod ipsorum forte recuperauerint / idem consanguineus noster et heredes sui habeant teneant et possideant seruicia heredum vel heredis dictorum thanorum vel thanj / et feodofirmas vel feodofirmam antiquitus debitas de thanagiis vel thanagio prenotatis / eisdem forma et consideracione / et pro seruiciis illis / quibus ipsa thanagia jam tenet aut tenere debet per infeodacionem nostram sibi alias inde factam / et prout carte nostre inde sibi confecte continent et proportant / In cuius rei testimonium ... Testibus ... apud Edynburghe / sexto die Maii / anno regni nostri quadragesimo (A.D. 1369).

Registrum Magni Sigilli Regum Scotorum, p. 66, No. 220.

APPENDIX No. XXIII.

WALTER LESLIE, EARL OF ROSS.

CHARTER by King DAVID II. to WILLIAM, Earl of Ross, of the Earldom of Ross, the Lordship of Sky, and all others his lands within the realm (except only the lordships and lands which sometime belonged to him by inheritance from MARGARET CUMYN, one of the heiresses of Buchan), in the Shires of Aberdeen, Dumfries, and Wigton, with remainder to WALTER LESLIE, knight, and EUFAMIA his spouse—A.D. 1370.

DAVID Dei gratia Rex Scottorum / omnibus . . . salutem / sciatis nos dedisse . . . dilecto consanguineo nostro Willelmo comiti de Ross / totum comitatum de Rosse / et dominium de Sky, ac omnia alia dominia et terras cum pertinentiis / que fuerunt ipsius comitis vbicunque infra regnum / exceptis dominiis illis et terris que fuerunt dicti comitis infra vicecomitatus de Abirdene / de Drumfres / et de Wygtona / Quem quidem comitatum / terras / et dominia cum pertinentiis / idem comes . . . . mera et spontanea voluntate sua / nobis apud Perth in pleno parliamento nostro tento ibidem vicesimo tertio dei mensis Octobris anno Domini Millesimo trecentesimo septuagesimo / in presencia Roberti Senescalli Scocie / comitis de Stratherne nepotis nostri / Willelmi comitis de Douglas / Georgii comitis Marchie / Johannis Senescalli comitis de Carryk / Archibaldi de Douglas / Roberti de Erskyne / Alexandri de Lindesay / Willelmi de Disschyngtona militum et aliorum plurium baronum et nobilium regni nostri per suas litteras patentes et eciam cum fusto et baculo per manus procuratorum suorum sufficientem ad hoc commissionem habentium sursum reddidit pureque et simpliciter resignauit . . . Tenenda et habenda dicto comiti et heredibus suis masculis de corpore suo legittime procreandis / quibus deficientibus / Waltero de

APPENDIX XXIII.

Lesley militi et Eufamie sponse sue ac eorum alteri diucius viuenti et heredibus de ipsa Eufamia legitime procreatis seu procreandis ita videlicet quod si heres masculus de ipsa Eufamia non exierit et plures forte de se habuerit filias / senior semper filia tam ipsius Eufamie quam suorum heredum de se excuntium deficientibus heredibus masculis habeat totum jus et integrum dictum comitatum dominia et terras cum pertinenciis exceptis supra exceptis, sine diuisione aliquali / Et ipsis Waltero et Eufamia sponsa sua et heredibus de ipsa Eufamia legitime procreandis fortasse deficientibus Johanna junior filia dicti comitis et heredes sui et quando ipsi heredes femelle fuerint semper senior heres femella sine diuisione et participatione aliqua / totum et integrum dictum comitatum dominia et terras predictas cum pertinenciis / exceptis supra exceptis / teneat et teneant / de nobis et heredibus nostris in feodo et hereditate / per omnes rectas metas et diuisas suas cum tenandriis seruiciis liberetenencium et aduacacionibus ecclesiarum / adeo libere et quiete in omnibus et per omnia sicut dictus Willelmus comes de Rosse consanguineus noster vel aliquis predecessorum suorum dictum comitatum dominia et terras predictas cum pertinenciis aliquo tempore liberius quiecius et honorificencius juste tenuit seu possedit / Faciendo inde seruicia debita et consueta / In cuius rei testimonium ... Testibus ... apud Perth / xxiij die Octobris anno regni nostri quadragesimo primo (A.D. 1370).

Registrum Magni Sigilli Regum Scotorum, p. 74, No. 258; and *Acts of the Parliaments of Scotland*, vol. i., app. p. 177; *Antiquities of Shires of Aberdeen and Banff*, vol. ii. p. 386.

APPENDIX.

APPENDIX No. XXIV.

WALTER LESLIE, EARL OF ROSS.

Appendix XXIV.

COMPLAINT to King ROBERT II., by WILLIAM, Earl of Ross, showing how the Earl's lands in Buchan, together with those of his Brother HUGH DE ROSS, were, without their consent, given by King DAVID II. to Sir WALTER LESLIE, Knight; and how the said Sir WALTER married the Earl's daughter EUPHAME, altogether against her Father's will—A.D. 1371.

1371.

EXCELLENTISSIMO principi ac domino suo reverendissimo / Domino Roberto Dei gratia Regi Scottorum / et suo bono concilio / vester humilis nepos Willelmus comes de Ross conqueritur sub hac forma / videlicet / Quod quondam bone memorie dominus meus Rex predecessor vester domino Waltero de Lesly militi ad impetrationem ejusdem dedit omnes terras meas et tenementa ac etiam fratris mei Hugonis de Ross infra Buchaniam existentes / me et fratre meo predicto non requisitis non citatis non in jure confessis nec in judicio convictis / Et cum constaret (michi) de saysina dictarum terrarum sic predicto Domino Waltero ex arupto et sine juris processu deliberata / scripsi domino Episcopo Brechynensi / tunc cancellario Scotie pro una litera attornatoria ex capella Regia continente has personas / videlicet / Robertum senescallum Scotie / dominos Thomam comitem de Mar / Willelmum de Keth, Willelmum de Meldrum / et singulis eorum singulariter unam literam clam supplicatoriam ut dignentur esse attornati ad petendum a domino meo Rege terras meas et fratris mei predicti ad plegium / una etiam cum una litera Domino meo Regi / et alia Domine Eufamie sorori mee / super eandem materiam ' Et cum predictis literis presentandis singulariter oneravi dominum Johannem de Gairdyn clericum meum canonicum Catanensem / cui itineranti occurreus Johannes de Aberkyerder / dicens se armigerum predicti Domini Walteri ipsum arrestavit hominemque suum atrocitur verberavit

APPENDIX XXIV.

quia magistrum suum ad eandam equi sui noluit ligare / ipsum de omnibus literis suis spoliavit et eum ad nemora et loca devia deduxit / De cujus arrestatione predictus clericus meus non potuisset deliberari quousque convenisset sibi sex marcas sterlingorum infra tres septimanas plegiis domino Roberto rectore de Forglen et Willelmo Byset de Routhyrlis / et fecit dictum clericum meum jurare super Sancta Evangelia presente Domino Cristino vicario de Forg quod non presentaret aliquam literam de eisdem alicui nisi pixidem cum dictis literis suo sigillo sigillatam Domino Waltero de Lesly domino suo / et quod intraret seipsum predicto Domino Waltero cum dicta pixide sigillata et sua litera / Quo facto predictus clericus sic deliberatus laboravit ad dominum suum Episcopum Aberdonensem conquerendo et ad dictum Dominum Willelmum de Keth qui ipsum de solutione pecunie predicte resolvebant / et ab hinc laboravit in Rossiam nuncians michi ista / Quo facto / sciens quod per medias personas literas meas ad plegium habere non potui / laboravi in propria persona ad dominum meum Regem usque villam de Aberdene ad petendum literas meas ad plegium / quas habere non potui nisi concedere (volui) predicto domino meo Regi pro usu Johannis de Logy totum jus meum de la Platan de Forfar / Cujus concessione facta vocatus ad prandium cum domino meo Regi petii responsum negotiorum meorum post prandium / a quo post avisationem suam missa fuit michi in ecclesia una magna sedula questionum pro responso / allegatis in eadem pluribus autoritatibus juris civilis / qua lecta dixi quod litiscontestationem facere nolui cum Domino meo Rege nec pro illa omnino veni / Et tunc nulla licentia petita ulteriori laboravi versus Rossiam nec plus cum predicto domino meo Rege usque adventum suum apud Inuernys loquebar / ubi percipientes predictum dominum meum contra me et fratrem meum Hugonem motum et dictum Dominum Walterum secum valde potiri / ego et frater meus Hugo predictus / ad statum pristinum et corporalem possessionem terrarum nostrarum Buchanie non restaurati / predictam donationem terrarum nostrarum predictarum factam per dominum Regem predicto Domino Waltero sub sigillis nostris ratificavimus propter pericula majora tunc eminentia ut estimavimus predicto fratre nostro tunc a nobis remoto in nemoribus et aliis deviis / Et non celando veritatem rei in re vera et fide qua Deo tenemur nec fuit filia nostra cum dicto Domino Waltero sponsata cum voluntate nostra sed omnino contra voluntatem nostram / nec aliquam concessionem vel donationem terrarum vel bonorum vel conventionem quamcunque sibi fecimus aliquo tempore usque diem obitus nostri Regis David predecessoris vestri / nisi ex rigore ejusdem domini Regis et sue iracundie timore / nullo tempore nostra spontanea voluntate bona ad hoc adhibita / Et hoc Deo et sue majestati celesti et vobis vestreque majestati terrestri innotescimus presenti scripto / In cujus rei testimonium presenti scripto sigillum meum est appensum / Datum apud Edynburgh vicesimo quarto die mensis Junii Anno Domini millesimo trecentesimo septuagesimo primo.

Antiquities of Shires of Aberdeen and Banff, vol. ii. p. 387. From a collection of Scottish Charters, MS., in the library at Panmure.

APPENDIX No. XXV.

WALTER LESLIE, EARL OF ROSS.

CHARTER by Sir WALTER LESLIE, Dominus de Ross, and EUPHAMIA his wife, to his Brother-in-law, Sir ALEXANDER FRASER, Knight, and JANET ROSS his wife, of the lands of Auchinschogle and Meikle Fyntra, in Buchan, and of other lands in Galloway and Ross, in full Exchange and Compensation for all claim of heritage in the lands of Ross, accruing to the said Sir ALEXANDER FRASER and JANET ROSS—A.D. 1375.

OMNIBUS hanc cartam visuris vel audituris ... Walterus Lesly miles dominus de Ross et Eufemia Ross sponsa sua. Salutem in Domino sempiternam. Noueritis nos unanimi consensu et assensu dedisse ... dilectis confratri et sorori

APPENDIX XXV.

nostre Alexandro Fraser militi et Jonete Ross sponse sue et eorum alteri diucius viuenti totas et integras terras meas de Auchinchogyle cum pertinentiis et terras meas de Meikle Fyntra cum pertinentiis jacentes in comitatu Buchanie infra vicecomitatum de Aberdene necnon terras nostras de Crekiltoun cum pertinentiis jacentes in dominio Gallvydie infra vicecomitatum de Wigtoun et annuum redditum octo decem librarum sterlingorum annuatim leuandum ... de totis et integris terris de Farindonald in Ross cum pertinentiis jacentibus infra vicecomitatum de Inuernes in merum liberum et legittimum excambium ac in recompensationem ... plenariam dictorum Alexandri militis et Jonete ac heredum suorum pro universis et singulis suis partibus hereditariis terrarum de Ross cum pertinentiis jacentibus infra vicecomitatum de Inuernes per dictos Alexandrum et Jonetam sponsam suam unanimi consensu et assensu pro se et heredibus suis sibi in excambium et contentationem nostrorum Walteri et Eufamie et heredum nostrorum pro dictis terris et annuo redditu nostris datis hereditarie et concessis Tenendas et habendas totas et integras terras predictas ... et annuum redditum ... dictis Alexandro et Jonete sponse sue et eorum alteri diucius viuenti et heredibus inter ipsos legittime procreatis seu procreandis quibus deficientibus heredibus legitimis dicte Jonete quibuscunque a nobis et heredibus nostris de supremo domino nostro Rege et successoribus suis in merum et legitimum excambium et contentationem antedictam in feodo et hereditate perpetuo ... Reddendo inde annuatim ... supremo domino nostro Regi ... seruicium dictarum terrarum et annui redditus debitum et consuetum ac wardam et releuium cum contingit ... In cuius rei testimonium sigillum meum presentibus est appensum apud Aberdeen quarto die mensis Junii Anno Domini millesimo ccc° septuagesimo quinto Testibus Willelmo Comite de Douglas Georgio de Dunbar Roberto Erskyne Willelmo de Dyschyntoun militibus et Thoma de Ret cum multis aliis.

1375.

Antiquities of Shires of Aberdeen and Banff, vol. ii. p. 350. From a collection of Scottish Charters, MS., in the library at Panmure.

APPENDIX No. XXVI.

EUFAMIA, COUNTESS OF ROSS.

CHARTER by EUPHAMIA, Domina de Ross, daughter and heiress of WILLIAM, Earl of Ross, to ANDREW MERCER, confirming the grant made to him by her husband, Sir WALTER LESLIE, deceased, Dominus de Ross, of the lands of Faythley and Tyrie in the Barony of Kynedward, and of certain yearly payments from the lands of Findlater, Netherdale, Pettendreich, and Culbirny, in the shire of Banff—A.D. 1382.

OMNIBUS hanc cartam visuris vel audituris / Eufamea domina de Rosse filia et heres Willelmi quondam comitis de Rosse / eternam in Domino salutem / Cum Joneta de Meyness filia et heres quondam Alexandri de Meyness domini de Forthyrgill . . . sua mera et spontanea voluntate in legittima sua viduitate existens / omnes et singulas terras de Faythley cum pertinentiis in baronia de Kynedward infra vicecomitatum de Aberden que fuerunt dicte Jonete / Karissimo domino nostro Domino Waltero de Lesley quondam sponso nostro et domino de Ross / per fustum et baculum sursum reddidit pureque et simpliciter resignavit / Et post modum dictus Dominus Walterus quondam sponsus noster / cum consensu et assensu nostro et ex maturo avisamento et distincta deliberatione concilii sui et nostri / predictas terras de Faythley cum pertinentiis dilecto consanguineo suo et nostro Andree Mercer ac heredibus suis et assignatis / pro servicio suo sibi et nobis impenso et in futurum impendendo / pro uno pare calcariorum deauratorum nomine albefirme heredibus dicti Domini Walteri sponsi nostri et nostris inter nos procreatis vel in posterum procreandis / nobis annuatim per predictum Andream heredes suos et assignatos tantum persolvendo / ac etiam dictus Dominus Walterus quondam maritus noster /

APPENDIX XXVI.

nostro etiam consensu et assensu / predicto Andree heredibus eius et assignatis novem libras sterlingorum de Fynleter / Natyrdole / et de Petyndreych / proportionaliter ac annuatim debitas / et viginti quatuor solidos de Culbreny annuatim debitos infra vicecomitatum de Banff / pro uno pare calcariorum deauratorum domino nostro Regi nomine albefirme annuatim tantum persolvendo per eundem Andream et heredes suos et assignatos / ac terras de Tyre cum pertinentiis in baronia de Kynedward infra vicecomitatum de Aberdeen / pro uno denario sterlingorum nomine albefirme per supradictum Andream heredes suos et assignatos nobis et heredibus nostris ut supra tunc annuatim persolvendo si petantur ... in perpetuum concessit / Nos vero / tandem nunc in nostra pura et legitima viduitate existens / predictas donationes ... dicti Domini Walteri quondam sponsi nostri de predictis terris de Faythley / et Tyry . et annuis redditibus de Finleter . Nathyrdole . Petyndreych / et de Culbreny / cum pertinentiis suis / de consensu et assensu nostro predicto Andree heredibus suis et assignatis factas / prout carte dicti Domini Walteri quondam sponsi nostri sibi inde facte plenius continent et testantur / in omnibus et per omnia ... et in perpetuum ratificamus ... In cuius rei testimonium sigillum nostrum presenti carte est appensum apud castrum nostrum de Dyngwale / nono die Mensis Martii Anno Domini Millesimo trecentesimo octuagesimo primo / His testibus venerabili in Christo patre domino Alexandro Dei gratia episcopo Rossensi / Magistro Willelmo de Digwale decano Rossensi / Waltero Senescalli / Ricardo Cumyne / militibus / Adam de Urchard vicecomite de Crombachy / Hugone de Munro / et multis aliis.

1381.

Antiquities of Shires of Aberdeen and Banff, vol. ii. p. 389. From a collection of Scottish Charters, MS., in the library at Panmure.

www.ingramcontent.com/pod-product-compliance
Lightning Source LLC
Chambersburg PA
CBHW020829230426
43666CB00007B/1155